All This and 10%

All This and 10%

JIM GODBOLT

ROBERT HALE · LONDON

© *Jim Godbolt 1976*

First published in Great Britain 1976

ISBN 0 7091 5841 6

Robert Hale Limited
Clerkenwell House
Clerkenwell Green
London ECIR OHT

Printed in Great Britain by Bristol Typesetting Co. Ltd,
Barton Manor, St. Philips, Bristol

CONTENTS

For Joan

ILLUSTRATIONS

ACKNOWLEDGEMENTS

The author wishes to express his appreciation to John Chilton, George Melly and Gordon M. Williams for reading successive drafts of this book and offering expert advice. That three established writers should spend valuable time assisting an unknown author is kindness itself and I am truly grateful.

I am particularly obliged to John Chilton for initially suggesting that I write this book. Before John's prompting it had not occurred to me that I should or could.

I am also grateful to Geoff and Joan Kemp and Campbell Burnap who read the book and gave advice, and to various individuals whose names appear throughout for giving permission for stories about them to be included. Without this readily imparted permission much of the book's substance would be lost.

I wish to give thanks to Ray Coleman, editor of the *Melody Maker*, for access to its files (and to Roy Burchall of that paper for finding me certain vital photographs) and Harold Pendleton, of the Marquee Organization, for allowing me to peruse the files of *Jazz News*, published by the National Federation of Jazz Organizations.

I acknowledge material from the magazine, *Jazz*, edited by James Asman and Bill Kinnell, the Humphrey Lyttelton Club newsletter and the *New Musical Express*. Finally I am obliged to Peter Clayton who gave the book a highly complimentary mention on the programme " Sounds of Jazz ", on B.B.C.'s Radio Two, before it had been accepted by Robert Hale.

Any author attempting a book of this nature needs the help of his friends, and in this regard I have been more than fortunate.

London, 1976   JIM GODBOLT

I

FEEL THE NOISE

In 1968, after nearly twenty years as a self-employed agent largely representing jazz bands, I was engaged as a booker of rock and roll groups by the Bron Organization, a management/agency/publishing/recording complex in Oxford Street.

I had no complaint with my boss, Gerry Bron, or my colleagues, but I was ill at ease in the larger context of the pop scene and in 1970, at the age of forty-eight, I decided to quit the music business completely. Not a decision of great historical moment—thousands quit jobs they do not like—but here I felt no longer able to continue the career, specialized in its own limited way, in which I was experienced. I felt a conflict between my private convictions and my booking responsibilities. I was selling music I did not like; nor did I like the aggravations with egocentric pop performers.

The artistes managed by Gerry Bron were mostly pleasant people, but the business generally had a fair proportion of monsters, many of whom we booked on behalf of our clients. We booked a much publicized group to play a ball for a fee of £750, a quite handsome figure for a one-hour spot. The group's management laid down a variety of contractual stipulations, one of them a lengthy clause obliging the sponsors to provide full security arrangements to safeguard the group from being mobbed by fans and their equipment from being burgled or damaged.

It was a reasonable enough stipulation, albeit one couched in terms more appropriate to the announcement of the Second Advent, but on the night of the engagement a security guard apprehended a drunk, dishevelled and ranting figure in the grounds round the venue. It was the leader of the group.

Inside the hall the group leader abused the guard and the organizing officials, threatened the guard with a fire axe and demanded that unless he were instantly dismissed the group would not play the engagement. He further insisted that one of the girl employees strip off, and ordered everyone else out of the room.

Denied this extra-contractual stipulation—I am sure his office had the omission of such a provision rectified in subsequent contracts—he demanded to be told the whereabouts of the lavatory. Advised of this, he decided it was too far for him to walk—he had had a tiring day—and urinated out of the window over passers-by.

The promoter could have justifiably cancelled the engagement but not with two thousand people in the hall who had paid to see the group and were unaware of back-stage dramas.

This is an unhappy dilemma for any promoter faced with such a situation and if the miscreant is a famous name with a drawing power he usually chooses to overlook the misdemeanours. The alternative is to disappoint his audience and himself lose money. The wayward demi-gods of the pop scene are very much aware of their power and as their egos are swollen by fulsome, sometimes hysterical, acclaim by public and press, it's no surprise they don't consider themselves to be ordinary mortals subject to the usual social restraints. The behaviour of this particular pop star was quite typical. Adulation, a dangerous drug, had gone to this pop star's head. Combined, as in this case, with liquid and inhaled stimulants, it made him above and beyond reason.

Such extreme behaviour wasn't that common, but more frequent than was good for business and, as my share was a percentage of gross turnover, I was particularly unhappy if these misdemeanours resulted in less commission or, when the group was sent back, none at all. My moral indignation about unprofessional behaviour became a fire of rage if I lost out financially.

I had a strong antipathy to the overwhelming volume at which most pop is played. When I had to listen to the groups, I hadn't the physical and nervous stamina to withstand the impact for any length of time. Never before has any kind of music been played at such sustained volume. Musicologists and psychologists may ponder the reasons for this phenomena; I can only record that I had to retreat when the decibel levels took me to the threshold of pain.

One of Bron's more famous groups is Uriah Heep. Typically, they carry an incredible amount of equipment. Their inventory comprises:

MAKE	ITEM
4 Dave Martin	Bass Bins
4 Dave Martin	Double Horn Units
3 Dave Martin	Single Horn Units
4 Dave Martin	Monitor Cabinets
2 Phase Linear	Power Amps
2 Allen & Heath	8 way mixer
1 Altec	BiAmplifier
1 W.E.M.	19 way multicore
2 Quad	Power Amps
1 Hammond (B74142)	B.3 organ and stool
2 Leslie	P.R.O. 900 cabinets
1 Moog (D1392E)	Mini Synthesiser
1 Simms-Watt	200 watt Amp
2 Simms-Watt	4 x 12 cabinets
5 Marshall	100 watt Amps
2 Marshall	4 x 12 Lead cabinets
2 Marshall	4 x 12 Bass cabinets
2 Acoustic	370 Amps GA 1009/1279
2 Acoustic	370 Speakers GB 1006/1019
2 Acoustic	271 Amps HA 1056/1062
2 Acoustic	271 Speakers HB 1001/1069
1 Acoustic	Amps GA 1280
2 Acoustic	Speakers GB 1091/1207
2 Fender	Champ Amps A31630/31672
1 Slingerland	Drum kit (chrome): Bass drum 24 x 14, Tom.-toms 20 x 18, 15 x 10, 14 x 10 + Hayman snare drums
3 Avedjis Zildian	Cymbals and Stands (22inch, 18inch, 15inch)
10 A.K.G.	D1000 microphones

MAKE	ITEM
2 A.K.G.	D12 microphones
8 Electrovoice	Microphones
1 Ludwig	Drum kit (Silver glitter): Bass drum 22 x 14, Tom-toms 12 x 8, 13 x 9, 16 x 16
1 Levin Acoustic	Guitar
1 Acoustic ' Black Widow '	,,
1 Gibson Les Paul	,,
1 Gibson SG (Cherry)	,,
1 Epiphone Custom (Sunburst)	,,
1 Martin Acoustic (Natural)	,,
1 Fender Jazz Bass (Natural)	,,
1 Yahama Acoustic Bass Fg300	,,
1 Gibson SG (Black)	,,
1 Fender Telecaster	,,
1 14 x 5 Hatman (gold lacquer)	Snare
1 Pr 15″ Avedis Zildian	Cymbal
1 Premier	Snare drum stand
1 Ludwig Speed King	Hi-hat pedal
1 Slingerland	Tom-tom holder
2 Ludwig	Cymbal stands
4 Slingerland	Spurs
2 Premier	Bass drum pedals
1 Premier	Stool
1 Ludwig	Anchor

4 tuning keys, 2 lengths of rope, 3 toolboxes.

Only the technically informed can fully grasp the significance of a list of gadgetry that cost £15,000, weighs five tons, takes two 3-ton vans to transport, and five ' roadies ' (road managers) six hours to set it up and another six hours to dismantle.

Uriah Heep comprises five musicians. On the road they have a team of seven to support them. Without these workhorses (some of them earning £5,000 a year) and this assembly of equipment, the group can't play a note.

That's a staggering thought for someone like myself, a jazz enthusiast brought up on the comparative simplicities of the jazz band's trumpet, trombone, clarinet and a three- or four-piece rhythm section, playing through one or two microphones, if that.

Moreover, this gargantuan equipment and the roadies are idle if one of the group is afflicted with a sore throat. Engagements worth up to a thousand pounds in this country and up to ten thousand in America (in vast stadiums and the like) have to be summarily cancelled because of the indisposition of the indispensable, another booking hazard in the pop scene.

Sheer volume is in itself an attraction to young people. " My kids like to feel the noise," claimed one promoter. Not all promoters can indulge their patrons in what some acoustic experts regard as a highly dangerous absorption of abnormal noise level. Some have to consider residential neighbours and include a clause in their contracts—the right to limit volume.

As a booker I used to reject offers that carried this stipulation. I knew that groups were psychologically as well as mechanically reliant upon electrical power and would resist entreaties from promoters to reduce the volume. They were incapable of performing without the surge of power to which they had grown accustomed.

Rightly or wrongly, I was highly critical of the influence of the rock and roll star, an influence often quite terrifying and out of proportion to intrinsic talents.

One, Rod Stewart, claimed in an interview printed in the *Melody Maker* that if he told his juvenile audience to " go and jump on the cops ", they would unquestionably obey. He was quite serious, and wholly believable.

This power brings considerable financial wealth. Stewart, for instance, bought himself a handsome property in Windsor set in spacious grounds for a reported figure of £90,000 and whilst many older people dislike rock and roll, disapprove of the performers' flowing locks and permissive attitudes, they are nevertheless impressed by their earning power and impact.

A pillar of the establishment, the B.B.C., is sufficiently impressed to allocate an inordinate amount of air-time to twittering and squawking disc jockeys presenting a ceaseless flow of pop records. It can't be denied that it's a testimony to the impact of modern pop that the B.B.C. with its long history of ' cultural ' programmes should be compelled to broadcast this ephemera so extensively.

In my objections to all these things I realized I was baying at the moon and, inconsistently and somewhat dishonestly, was a part of the scene in which they flourished.

When I tried rationally to assess my hostile reactions to certain musical and social trends, I was acutely aware that with the stiffening of the arteries comes a rigidity of attitude to things beyond my understanding. I was aware that the generation (and a half) gap was a yawning artistic as well as social chasm. Like a lot more middle-aged people, I see rock and roll as a noisome symptom of an increasingly unsettled and tormented era.

But I had to remind myself that in protesting the value of jazz music and scoffing at the ' corny ' tastes of my elders in the late 1930s, I was also part of a rebellion, albeit one of limited scale. It had none of the profound sociological implications of today's changes—nor did we have papers like *Oz* and *International Times* with their anti-establishment irreverence and sexual candour to support our ' rebellious ' philosophies. Our bible then, the *Melody Maker*, was an establishment paper, very much for King and Country and the *status quo*.

In 1970, after two years with the Bron Organization, I was, in a typically middle-aged manner, making useless comparisons with the time I first came into the music business. This was in 1946, and with associations going back to 1940.

Then it was a *very* different scene.

2

THAT NOISE WILL DRIVE YOU MAD

I entered the entertainment business by accident. The outcome has been largely stimulating, sometimes lucrative, frequently otherwise, and constantly aggravating. It's also had its very funny moments.

After a dead-end job as a stockbroker's office boy, followed by naval service, I became manager of a jazz band and subsequently drifted into being an agent.

There are no courses to study on how to become an agent any more than there are on how to become a second-hand car salesman. I've never heard of any boy expressing the wish to become an agent when he grows up and I wouldn't recommend that the idea is put into any young head. There are many less hazardous and nerve-racking ways of earning a living.

Not that I'm complaining. Many have drifted into jobs infinitely less absorbing and entertaining than the one I had for twenty years. Without any scholastic or technical qualifications, it was a happy quirk of fortune to have, for the most part, earned more money than I would have received at an office or factory, although my income has frequently been below the national average. It has been a see-saw existence.

Up to the time I became an agent I had only a vague idea of how one functioned and this was culled from pre-war British films seen from the ninepenny seats of the local Odeon.

These films featured stars from a then thriving variety business and the stories based on real-life situations. The agent was portrayed as a somewhat excitable character, perhaps rather shady, always corpulent, often Jewish, and the casting couch was conveniently situated near his enormous desk.

B

This rather unsavoury image of a hustling, cigar-smoking middle man exploiting honest troupers was to continue after the war when the music halls went into unhappy decline. Jazz bands became the troupers, touring clubs and *palais* up and down the country.

In the mid 'forties and early 'fifties, jazz was as much an ideology as a music. It was first played by the oppressed negro in the United States and there was much identification with this state of oppression and separateness by pale-faced youths from Sidcup to Wallasey, who had become jazz musicians, and any-one, an agent for instance, seeming to take advantage of these, was a villain – at best a necessary evil. This is an attitude not uncommon amongst performers in all branches of the entertainment industry.

In 1950 I became one of these necessary evils when I started in business representing only jazz bands. No dance orchestras, singers or sundry entertainers. These I came to represent later, often disastrously.

From the mid 'thirties the real history of jazz was being thoroughly researched and interest in this previously abused, misrepresented and emasculated music was now centred on the genuine article.

It was the new ' Jazz Age ', the term having more significance than when first coined in the 'twenties. Jazz flowered in that decade but the music associated with the ' Jazz Age ' had the most tenuous connection with jazz. It was mostly corny dance music, highly arranged, jerkily syncopated and largely without improvization.

The interest in true jazz owed much to the activities of record collectors mostly in England and France. In the 'thirties they met almost clandestinely in their ' dens ' to play treasured records, often in the teeth of intense opposition from the rest of the family, long conditioned by the radio and gramophone to the sweet music of the dance bands so much ' a rage ' in the 'twenties and 'thirties. They thought ethnic jazz a strident, un-musical cacophony, only to be expected of the primitive negro.

In the 'twenties a painter called John B. Soutar exhibited a picture at the Royal Academy. It portrayed a naked white girl peering into the heavens. Seated next to her on the torso of a broken classical statue was a negro. Dressed in formal evening wear—top hat, white tie and tails—he was playing a saxophone.

The title of the picture was " Breakdown ". The symbolism was obvious. Civilization was in decline and ' Jazz ' was contributing to the decay. There was an indignant editorial in the *Melody Maker*, the musicians' trade paper. Under the stern heading " Problems Of An Immodest Masterpiece " it said, " We must repudiate the inference to be drawn from this juxtaposition of an undraped white girl with a black man. It is a slap in the face for modern dance music. Such a study is straining beyond breaking point the normal clean inference of allegory. We demand also that this habit of associating our music with the primitive and barbarous negro shall cease forthwith, in justice to the fact that we have outgrown such comparisons."

This impassioned protest came from an allegedly ' jazz ' paper. What then was the layman to think? The *Melody Maker*'s reference to " our music " was the corny dance music of the 'twenties, mistakenly described as jazz, as was similar although more sophisticated, dance music of the 'thirties and 'forties. This was the very misconception the jazz collectors and critics arduously campaigned to change in the correspondence columns of the *Melody Maker*, in specialist home-produced magazines and by pressing the record companies to issue, or re-issue jazz classics of the 'twenties. They formed rhythm clubs to meet and play records and by 1940 some critics were fervently proclaiming that New Orleans jazz was the source and the essence of the music.

During the mid 'forties in England, particularly, young record collectors had become musicians with a passionate and single-minded desire to play in the New Orleans idiom. Until then there had been several excellent British jazzmen but their models were mostly the ' swing ' soloists of the 'thirties, like clarinettist Benny Goodman and trumpeter Harry James. They played mostly in dance bands.

Those professionals were scornfully regarded by the New Orleans purists; in like fashion they condemned a potent new jazz development—Be-Bop—a completely new manner of improvizing that was challenging the old modes that were being so strenuously revived. Jazz in all its aspects had never enjoyed such public interest, never aroused such controversy before.

This was the immediate background of my entry into the business.

The most significant, and for a time, the most famous of the English disciples of New Orleans jazz to play in that idiom were George Webb's Dixielanders. There were a few other bands of similar character active but none had the storming impact of the Webb band. They had the traditional instrumentation of trumpet, trombone, clarinet, drums, piano and banjo. Their repertoire was the tunes of the New Orleans pioneers, the style a combination of solo and collective improvization in the fashion of their models.

Quite astonishing, then, was the seeming authenticity of their music. Of course, it wasn't authentic. This could only be said of the American original but in those heady days of romantic revivalism the Dixielanders had the *quality* of authenticity. They were utterly dedicated to absorbing the soul and essence of early jazz, nothwithstanding their technical limitations. In our eager acceptance of these sturdy pioneers' principles, we overlooked their faulty technique. Many regarded these deficiencies as virtues and some of us were using such phrases as " contrapuntal interplay " when talking about their collective improvization.

The Webb band deliberately rejected the band uniforms worn by their dance band contemporaries. They had no music stands. They'd have been superfluous. Only one of them could read music.

Despite the emotional impact they made in this completely sincere attempt to absorb the musical language of another social culture of a time past, they were not entirely successful in their aims. They hadn't the musicianship of their inspirations, nor was their environment anything like the Afro-American culture that spawned jazz at the turn of the century.

George Webb's Dixielanders' real significance was in spearheading a movement that was to considerably alter the pattern of the popular music industry in this country, notably during the 'fifties but with results still to be seen today in the bands of

Acker Bilk, Kenny Ball, Chris Barber, Alex Welsh, Alan Elsdon, Monty Sunshine and many more.

The Dixielanders played every Monday evening in the garden basement of a pub called ' The Red Barn ' in Barnehurst, Kent, the headquarters of the Bexleyheath and District Rhythm Club founded during the war.

Barnehurst, a typical 'thirties subtopian estate development, was half-an-hour's train journey from Charing Cross, and the most unlikely Mecca for the spawning of revivalist jazz, but that basement was packed every week with enthusiastic upholders of the faith listening to this out-of-tune band playing blues, rags, stomps and marches. Rumbustious ensembles and soaring improvizations came within earshot of ' Mon Repos ', ' Thistle-dome ' and ' Dunroamin ' nearby, a *milieu* so many thousands of miles away and so utterly different in character from Lulu White's Mahogany Hall and other New Orleans sporting houses where so much early jazz was played. The pilgrimage to these sessions had a romantic, almost evangelical fervour.

Local dance band musicians, themselves improvizers if the opportunity arose, were very critical. They complained about the old-fashioned conception, the poor intonation, the vocalized tones and some claimed that they, too, could play in that anti-quated manner if they so wanted.

Generally, this wasn't true. With all their superior technique they hadn't the feel for the music the Dixielanders were playing.

At the same time there was a group of professional musicians, the Vic Lewis-Jack Parnell Jazzmen, playing in a similar style. They recorded for a major company, broadcast regularly and made a lot of public appearances, but, lacking the Webb Band's patent dedication and conviction, they didn't impress, soon disbanded and the personnel returned to the palais' dance bands.

(It's ironic that, in 1972, the Lewis-Parnell band were represented in an anthology of British jazz to commemorate the B.B.C.'s fiftieth birthday, but Webb's Dixielanders, who also made broadcasts, were not. The Lewis-Parnell recordings are, in the passage of time, preferable, but this doesn't detract from the historical truth that it was the Webb band that made the tremendous emotional impact and dramatically led the revival.)

Another revivalist band of the time was led by trumpeter

Freddy Randall. The purists considered them to be flashy *and*
they played ' White ' jazz in contrast to the Dixielanders' superior
' Coloured ' style. Randall's Band came from Walthamstow, East
London, and the Dixielanders from the opposite side of the river.
The geographical distance was also an artistic and ideological
gap. Dotty days. . . .

The Dixielanders were formed in 1943. In 1945 chance nudged
me into hearing them. During my naval service I had kept in
touch with jazz collectors and writers I'd met before call-up.
One of them, Max Jones, was then editing a private monthly
magazine called *Jazz Music* (the organ of the Jazz Sociological
Society of Great Britain!) and had recently joined the *Melody
Maker* staff.

One leave I went to see Max with a story I had written about
my discovering a veritable Aladdin's Cave of rare 78 rpm records
in a Cape Town hardware shop.

Jazz record collectors have long sought rare records in junk
shops and this haul must rank as one of the greatest ever.

They were almost all rarities on labels that had never been
issued in England and were in mint condition. The labels alone
sent my blood racing. Paramount, Cameo, Vocalion, Emerson,
Harmony, Okeh, Banner, BlueBird, Victor . . . and the artistes
. . . Blind Lemon Jefferson, Lil Armstrong, Dixie Syncopators,
Louisiana Five, Clarence Williams, John Williams Synco Jazzers,
Will Ezell, The Washingtonians, Blind Blake, Lonnie Johnson . . .
it was like wandering into a jazz collector's Eden.

I bought about 150 at a shilling apiece and deviously wangled
them past an obdurate Afrikaans Customs Officer in Cape Town
harbour and stowed them aboard my ship, H.M.S. *St Zeno*, a
converted Hull trawler. Thanks to the devoted thoroughness in
the way I packed them, they eventually made the journey home
in a troop ship without a single breakage.

Nowadays the financial value of this incredible find would
run into hundreds of pounds, rare jazz records fetching as much
as fifty pounds. That's a sobering thought, having virtually sold
this treasure haul to counter successive financial crises, one of
many actions I deeply regret.

After I had given this story to Max, he sadly told me he *had* to go and listen to some so-called 'New Orleans' band called George Webb's Dixielanders. We exchanged knowing looks but both of us were due for a shock. He at a club in London and me, weeks later, at 'The Red Barn'.

When I first heard the Dixielanders, I was utterly overwhelmed by their sound and what I thought it signified. It was like a divine revelation. I vaguely remember gushing my appreciation to George and he gave me a typically quizzical look. I was un-doubtedly over-rapturous in my admiration, my rapture prob-ably inflamed by several glasses of mild and bitter at one shilling a pint.

I was surprised to find that I knew the band's clarinettist, Wally Fawkes, and equally surprised to find he had become a musician.

In 1941 Wally and I were members of the 161 Rhythm Club, so-called because it was 160th in formation after the founding of the No 1 Rhythm Club in 1933, under the sponsorship of the *Melody Maker*. Jazz being synonymous with nameless depravity, I entered this Bacchanalian abandonment of moral values every Monday evening at the Station Hotel, Sidcup, Kent, where the club—maximum attendance of nine—met and listened to records played on a portable turntable plugged into the electric light socket.

The club room, above the saloon bar, was rented to us for five shillings a session and the strains of hot jazz filtered through blacked-out windows to mingle with the more sinister noises of aeroplane drone, bombs falling and bursts of ack-ack fire. We drank very little, but when we did mild and bitter was seven-pence a pint, scotch eightpence a nip (old pence of course).

Some of the pub's regulars, particularly the residents of 'old' Sidcup (the Victorian, as opposed to the newly developed 'sub-topian' part) regarded the sounds from our gramophone with almost as much apprehension as the battle noises outside. Our sessions were solemn affairs. Jazz was a serious matter that called for avid listening and profound comment. We would take it in turns to give 'recitals' followed by fierce and asinine debates, with me heavy on the asinine. No mock self-denigration here. It's an unfortunate characteristic of my middle-age that I am acutely embarrassed by crystal-clear recollections of my adolescent behaviour and attitudes.

Our recital subjects were " Negro *v.* White ", " Chicago *v.* New York " (' New Orleans ' was a style almost unknown to us) or there would be a programme devoted to one instrumentalist, band or instrument. Youthfully eager, we sat around a long table, heads nodding and Oxford bags flapping as we tapped our feet to the beat. From ' sports ' jackets worn over patterned pullovers we took Woolworth's sixpenny fountain pens to make urgent notes.

Formative days! In the 'thirties and 'forties, rhythm clubs were the stamping ground of the ' hot cognoscenti ' and in 1941 the famous magazine *Picture Post* carried a feature on a rhythm club, showing earnest devotees listening to a ' jam session ' with utter absorption. At least *Picture Post* acknowledged that jazz fans were serious about their music. Serious we most certainly were. Deadly, comically, serious.

We were an underground movement. There was a pristine spirit of romance, the adventure of discovering new musical joys on record, and these were rare enough as the record companies issued only one jazz record a month.

Six months or so before I went into the Navy, I gave up my office job to work on a building site and having more cash to spare I ventured from Swinging Sidcup to the dimmed lights of the West End to attend meetings of the No. 1 Rhythm Club. I was star-struck at meeting famous jazz ' experts ' whose names appeared in the feature pages and the correspondence columns in the *Melody Maker* each week. I dared not talk to musicians. That would have been too much of a presumption.

A great honour was accorded me by the club's secretary and founder, Bill Elliot, a most affable man. He asked me to act as one of the stewards at the first ever recorded ' Public Jam Sessions ' to be held at E.M.I. Studios in St John's Wood in November 1941. I was flattered beyond belief and lorded it over my fellow members of the 161 Rhythm Club, especially as the *Melody Maker* carried the story that the stewards had been *chosen* from various rhythm clubs. The 161 was mentioned but, to my intense disappointment, my name wasn't, though it was included in the programme notes. I was thrilled until I looked more closely and noticed that I was given as Jimmie Codbolt. Still, I thought, those present would know who I was. Hadn't my name appeared as secretary of the 161 Club in our weekly notice? And what of the ' controversial ' article I had published in the *Melody Maker* in June that year? (It was now November but surely they'd remember?).

The *Melody Maker* didn't acknowledge receipt of this article, but more important, printed it. As usual I bought the paper one Friday morning on my way to work and was thrilled to see my first-ever article in print and read it and re-read it on the No. 44 tram to Southwark Bridge, fourpence return, workman's ticket.

Feeling very pleased with myself, I must have read it five thousand times that weekend and the *Melody Maker* sent me two guineas, which was twelve shillings more than I was getting for my weekly wage as the City's oldest office boy.

The *Melody Maker*, now fifty years of age, was vastly different in those days in style and content. It was primarily the journal of the dance band musicians, although jazz was given good coverage and it was considerably more informed on the subject than in 1926, when they slated John Soutar's " immodest masterpiece ".

Its phraseology, now quaintly archaic, included references to " Ace Saxophonist " Art Christmas, " Keyboard Wizard " or " Ivory Tickler " for pianist Gerry Moore, " Nimble-fingered Claryist " for Nat Temple and " Swing Canary " for vocaliste Gwen Jones.

They were fond of the headline, " Bombshell Hits The Profession ", alluding to nothing more explosive than, say, a violinist and orchestra leader Sydney Simone, not exactly a household name, leaving a West End restaurant after a long residency.

The *Melody Maker*, bless it, got into a proper wax when a lady announcer on the B.B.C. made a disparaging remark about a jazz record. The lady's gaffe was construed as " An insult to swing fans throughout the country ". They demanded, and received, an apology from the B.B.C.

The paper cost tuppence and although reduced in size because of paper rationing, it proudly carried on as " spokesman for the profession " and was up in arms over slurs in the national press that dance band musicians were evading call-up.

One night there was a flutter of excitement at the 161 Rhythm Club. A local band leader dropped in, accompanied by a girl. She looked glamorous, as befitted a bandleader's lady. She sat in a corner, bored and aloof. A record, " Shim-Me-Sha-Wobble ", by a band called Miff Mole and His Molers was played and during an agitated solo by ' Chicagoan ' clarinettist Frank Teschmaker she emitted a shriek of horror and fled the room.

Teschmaker's playing was indeed shrill and dissonant, but this wasn't the reason for her screaming departure. She had idly looked up to see a large spider crawling down the wall. As secretary of the club I bought her a glass of port to steady her nerves when she returned, weepily, to the club room, and I charged the cost, fivepence, to club expenses.

Wally and I lived in the subtopian part of Sidcup, and walked home together. He was a quiet young man and I, a very garrulous young man, did all the talking. If an air raid was in progress, we would back against the nearest wall, but only when injury seemed imminent did we raise our precious discs of shellac above our heads as protection from shrapnel hissing down from the skies. When I got home I'd maybe play a record I had borrowed that night, or a ' find ' discovered in a pile of 78s in a junk store and purchased for a few coppers. My father loathed jazz and his features would contort with pain as it assailed his ears. He warned me, " That noise will drive you mad ". He couldn't understand my liking for something that " hadn't got a tune to it ". He was wrong that jazz was without tune and, productive of insanity or not, it was to play a large part in my life and for many years it was my living, starting with me becoming the Dixielanders' manager after a few months as their number one hanger-on.

In the dog days of my naval service, I artfully contrived to get myself on a gunnery course at Whale Island, Portsmouth, and I constantly travelled up to London to listen to the band, even at rehearsals. I didn't learn a thing about gunnery. My thoughts were on getting up to Barnehurst to hear the band that, to me, was Messianic in its propagation of the gospel of New Orleans Jazz.

3

JAZZ AND ONLY JAZZ

Shortly after demobilization I became the Dixielanders' manager. Correction—George Webb didn't like the term ' manager ' : and I became the band's general factotum, for three pounds a week, with the title of ' secretary '. I was also the whipping boy for two members of the band.

I mention this animosity as my first experience of many musicians' attitudes towards non-playing functionaries. The banjo player, particularly, had a long nose for my faults, but was extremely obsequious to George. He wore a perpetual smile (except when addressing me) to display overtly a fine set of teeth (which he managed to expose even when smoking a pipe), making me forever wary of individuals with a constant beam.

George was a chirpy, forceful character and quite ferocious when aroused. He had considerable strength of character, and kept the band together for five years. He received very little financial reward for his pioneering endeavours and many who made large sums out of the trad jazz boom of the 'fifties owe much to his push and determination in the trail-blazing 'forties.

It was very difficult to obtain engagements for the band. Concert and dance promoters were wary of a band so uncompromising. " Jazz and Only Jazz " was their slogan and they meant it. Some promoters realized their intransigence only when their customers were demanding " something they could dance to ". They didn't repeat the booking. It was a standing joke in the band that they had played every hall in the area—once.

In their zealous determination to spread the gospel of ' true ' jazz they remained steadfast. It was ' Us ' against ' Them '.

One engagement was in a West End theatre with some dance-

cum-' swing ' bands. To save time in the change-overs the promoters dictated that the Dixielanders' front-line—now two trumpets, trombone and clarinet—play with the rhythm section of
another band on the concert. This was quite unacceptable!
What could these slick, *professional* musicians with all their
facile technical ability know about the complexities of New
Orleans-style contrapuntal interplay?

Harry Hayes, a pioneer jazz saxophonist, but mostly active in
dance bands, was the musical director of the show. I called on
him at his instrument shop in Shaftesbury Avenue to advise
firmly that the Dixielanders couldn't possibly appear without
their own rhythm section. Hayes, more interested in selling saxophones than listening to my objections, curtly dismissed me with
the information that chords are chords whoever plays them and
was emphatic that the rhythm section selected could easily handle
the *simple* chord sequences of the Dixielanders' repertoire. Such
was the extent of my naïvety and strong antipathy towards individuals who couldn't grasp the significance of the Dixielanders'
music, I walked out of his shop astounded beyond belief, quite
convinced that Hayes had no conception of true jazz.

George turned the job down. United they stood. . . .

The band played monthly concerts at the Congregationalist
Memorial Hall in Farringdon Street, near St Pauls. It was a
cold and forbidding barn of a place, not really suitable as a jazz
venue. The concerts were sponsored by *Challenge*, the organ of
the Young Communist League who backed jazz as a proletarian
art form and presented it as the language of the oppressed.

This party line had little relevance to these young men from
London's suburbia, but the Y.C.L. were indeed good friends of
the band. These concerts gave them badly needed exposure in
Central London. The programme comprised a recital of jazz
records by a well-known critic, followed by the band's session.
Busts of grim-visaged Congregationalist notables long dead
looked from high-arched windows on a spectacle their models
would have surely abhorred, but in the late 'forties the music
from these scruffily dressed individuals on the stage had an
appeal pertinent to the time. Many, not particularly interested
in jazz or its ideologies, found the music a happy noise in the
grey post-war era of food rationing and general shortage.

Much had been written about the band. Max Jones, after reluctantly going to hear them, foresaw that their influence would mean a departure from the usual assembly of saxophones and a rhythm section, then common in jazz clubs, playing endless choruses on 'standards' like "Dinah" and "Lady Be Good". His prophecies proved to be correct.

Before I became officially connected with the band I wrote a glowing appreciation in the *Melody Maker* under the heading " Jazz in Surburbia " : " Although their outmoded style is put over with inherent musicianship the players are not musicians in the acceptable sense of the word. They are *enthusiasts* first with an enthusiast's outlook. That's an important distinction. It explains the enormous difference between these few players and the swing-blinded majority with their sterile riffs and interminable choruses on " Doggin' Around " and " Tea For Two " and their ' jamming ' instead of real group improvization."

A lot of muddled thinking went into those angular phrases but the sentiments were then thought to be gospel truth by the band's small but fervent bunch of supporters.

Before this the English critic, James Asman, had repeatedly lauded them in his magazine *Jazz*, but in the same publication another critic, Stanley Dance, reviewed the first Webb record and made some trenchant remarks about the concept of revivalism. He asserted it was not natural to the time. He had a " mistrust of an artificial return to original simplicities ". He argued that looking back for artistic inspiration was historically and musically untenable and he wagged an admonitory finger about the solos on the record. " And those solos! What about the old polyphony and them there polyrhythms? Play the game you cats!" He was having a little gentle fun at the expense of those critics (one of them his editor) who used such terminology, especially those who dogmatically asserted that collective improvization was infinitely superior to solo flights of improvization. But this astringent criticism from a perceptive critic in a magazine of limited issue didn't in any way dam the flow of revivalism and it soon flourished in the shape of many bands and clubs throughout the country.

The Dixielanders held their first rehearsals in the drawing-room of the Webbs' home in Bexleyheath, near Barnehurst, much to the chagrin of George Webb Senior who described the noise as " filthy jizz "—amongst stronger epithets. George's mother, a lady of exceptional grace and dignity took the events in her stride and supplied refreshments for these young revolutionaries. Sadie Webb, possessing a rare warmth and generosity of spirit, was one of the most lady-like women I have ever met. I stayed with the Webbs for a while and she was like a mother to me.

Most of the band worked in the Vickers Armstrong factory in nearby Crayford and Wally Fawkes, who initially tuned his clarinet by dropping pieces of string into the mouthpiece, was drawing ' column-breakers ' for the *Daily Mail* under the pseudonym of ' Trog '.

First jokily billed as Spider Webb and his Cobs, the band made their debut at ' The Red Barn '. They soon became the resident band, added another trumpet and, later, a sousaphone. The most influential band in the British ' New Orleans ' revival was born and two years later I was fervently, emotively, involved.

Youthfully enthusiastic, they played on buses and trains on the way to engagements delighting in the astonished reaction. I travelled with the band to Derby where they made records for *Jazz*, Britain's first independent record label, run by James Asman and Bill ' Fu ' Kinnell.

In the scramble for seats in an overcrowded train, the band piled into a first-class carriage and were soon playing. The bell of Eddie Harvey's trombone was within inches of a full Colonel seated, ramrod fashion, in a reserved corner seat. The Colonel took this unexpected entertainment stoically, didn't say a word or raise an eyebrow, but alighted at the next stop obviously to find another seat, it being certain he was no jazz fan. The ticket collector, overwhelmed by the novelty—especially the sousaphone—forgot to make the excess charge.

At the recording session I held Roy Wykes' bass drum to prevent it from ' creeping ' and gave an enthusiastic yell at the end of the recording. Kinnell severely admonished me and George gave me one of his crushing scowls. My exultant cry was not to be permanently etched on record. It was cut.

The band played an engagement at a local town hall, sharing the bill with a local dance-cum-swing band dressed in formal wear known as monkey-suits. The Dixielanders were dressed in whatever had taken their fancy and some of them didn't have much of a wardrobe to choose from. George Webb had taken off his jacket, displaying his braces.

During a lively stomp from the Dixielanders one of the dance band waggled a glove puppet from behind the back-drop curtain. Only George, playing piano side-on, noticed this. A small stocky man, with little fear in his make-up and not one to argue the rights and wrongs of a matter where more direct methods would suffice, he arose from the piano stool, strode over and landed a hefty blow on the outline of the puppet-waggler whilst the band played on. The puppet disappeared from sight and the curtain puckered wildly as the joker grabbed it to save himself from falling. George returned to the piano stool and recommenced playing. The mocker had acted unprofessionally and was summarily punished. George's words on the matter, growled in a strong cockney accent were brief. " He was a bleedin' liberty-taker, won'e ?"

Apart from the ebullient George there were other rare characters in the band. Owen Bryce, second trumpet and founder member, was a strict vegetarian who walked, sockless, out-of-doors in the coldest of weather. He wore a pair of brown corduroy trousers that came almost up to his nipples. He had a large upturned nose and was dubbed, amongst other things, Cyrano.

He came in for a lot of ribbing. It bounced off him. His ego, largely deprived of praise, fed on antipathy. He had a fine conceit of himself and was severely astringent in his criticism of others. He made few exceptions in this blanket criticism of the human race. It was he who stood alone. He worked extremely hard to make his record and radio shop a deserved success and although an avowed socialist, he sanctimoniously preached honest endeavour and self-reliance with the fervour of a Samuel Smiles. Owen was a very Smilesian man.

He had a withering contempt for our ' incorrect ' diet, a missionary zeal to convert us all to vegetarianism. Every morning, winter and summer, he would go for a swim in the local baths,

A meeting of West Hampstead Rhythm Club, 1941, featured in
Picture Post. The caption read, "The audience is young and intense
and with rapt attention they follow the trombonist's variations on a
jazz theme. Their talk is of 'hot breaks'. 'Bix', 'Tram' and 'Teagarden' are the names of their gods." *(Photo: Radio Times Hulton)*

George Webb's Dixielanders at 'The Red Barn', Barnehurst, Kent,
1946. *Left to right:* Eddie Harvey, Owen Bryce, Reg Rigden, Wally
Fawkes, Buddy Vallis and George Webb; *behind:* Derek Bailey and
Art Streatfield

The Dixielanders with singer Beryl Bryden and the author *(top right)*
(Photo : Beryl Bryden)

Sidney Bechet with Humphrey Lyttelton's Band, Winter Gardens
Theatre, London, November 1949. *Left to right :* Bechet, Ian Christie,
Wally Fawkes and Humphrey Lyttelton *(Photo : Associated Newspapers
Group Ltd.)*

emerge, have a hot shower and plunge straight back into the pool. The band vehemently refused his insistent invitations to join him in this health-giving exercise, nor were they enthusiastic about the nut cutlets, raw vegetables and dandelion coffee so much a part of his diet. They were in stupefied awe when he totally fasted for up to a month's duration. Like most fervent missionaries, his terminology rationalized his beliefs. If I had a boil on my neck, I was eating the wrong foods. If he had a boil on his neck, there were the poisons coming out thanks to a correct diet. Against such sophistry it was hard to win. He wasn't averse to advertising himself. He had the following intelligence printed in large letters on a poster strung across his delivery van:

OWEN BRYCE! WHO IS THIS MAN? BRITAIN'S FIRST JAZZ TRUMPETER! COMPOSER! ARRAN-GER! TALENT-SPOTTER! BAND-LEADER! BUSI-NESS MAN! FARMER! FAMILY MAN!

In a duplicated hand-out from his office, the text, headed "THE OWEN BRYCE EPIC", outlined the extent of his considerable achievements.

He belonged to the Woolwich Chamber of Commerce and frequently astounded his fellow members. In an after-lunch speech he told them they were all "selfish and inefficient". He added, "I don't waste time like most people. I don't clean my finger-nails. I bath once a month. Seldom do I go for a haircut and when I do I usually work out something in my mind whilst I'm in the barber's chair."

In a report of this speech in a local newspaper, the reporter added that local business men sat "mouths agape" and some looked "aghast". Understandably so: characters like Owen Bryce were not encountered every day of the week, and the references to his uncleanliness were intended to shock, and not the least bit true.

I admired and liked Owen and was considerably influenced by him. Despite his massive egotism he was a staunch, honest individual, although my faith in his vegetarianism was consider-ably strained when he became a pig breeder.

Despite occasional upsets I got on well with trombonist Eddie

C

Harvey. He developed tastes and aspirations outside the limited
style of the Dixielanders. He played in local dance bands to gain
experience and this shocking, almost traitorous deviationism
showed in his playing.

A meeting, ostensibly to discuss band matters, was called,
but it was really an inquisitorial council to pass judgement on
Eddie for straying from the paths of righteousness. Such was
the parochial rigidity of our thinking in those days, we demanded
that this nefarious practice of playing with *dance* bands cease
forthwith.

Eddie was shortly to be called up and was replaced by Harry
Brown whose style was more in keeping with the band's funda-
mentalist policy. He, too, soon received his calling-up papers.
In both cases I engaged in lengthy correspondence with the
Ministry of Labour, pleading they were highly specialized musicians and quite irreplaceable. The authorities were oddly unimpressed and both went into the R.A.F.

Wally Fawkes was the star of the band. His warm tone and
free flowing line inspired by the great New Orleans clarinettists
merited much praise. Tall, lantern-jawed and laconic, he was
considerably more sophisticated than the rest of us. Working
for a national newspaper and much admired for his clarinet
playing, his personality had matured considerably from the time
I had previously known him as the quiet sixteen-year-old at the
161 Rhythm Club. Success had given him a relaxed confidence.
He had the air of a young man who knew he was going to be a
success in life.

George Webb's Dixielanders were a collection of idiosyncratic
characters fiercely intransigent in their musical policy. It was
their biggest asset, and made the impact they so thoroughly
deserved.

After disagreements with the Young Communist League, we
started promoting our own concerts once a month under the
name of the " Hot Club of London " firstly at the Victoria Hall,
Bloomsbury, and later at King George's Hall, headquarters of
the Y.M.C.A. in Gt Russell Street.

Both had proper stage amenities and if I deserve praise for
anything during my stint as the band's factotum it was for find-

ing these venues in war-damaged London and talking the managers into letting us use them. I had to be wary of mentioning jazz. It was still a dirty word, partly due to Fleet Street's unremitting misreporting of jazz events and jazz people. I claimed we were a music club and careful not to say what sort of music.

George Webb Snr, now using slightly less scurrilous epithets to describe " filthy jizz " used to drive us and the equipment to and from the venue in an ancient Ford. One night as we stopped at a traffic light not far from the West End, a long, low, glistening coupé drew up alongside. At the wheel was Noel Coward, presumably on his way to his country house at Godstone after finishing a show. Elegant young men with fluffy poodles on their knees lounged in the passenger seats. Webb Snr, a barrel-chested man with strong, gnarled features put his head out of the window, slapped the side of his battered vehicle and addressed Coward in a rich Cockney accent, " Swop yer?" he shouted and Coward roared with laughter. It was an unexpected and highly comic confrontation between two entirely different people—from every possible point of view—and the cameo is etched in my memory.

In January 1947 we heard of a trumpeter of exceptional ability playing every Sunday at a pub called ' The Orange Tree ' at Friern Barnet, North London. It was reported, almost in hushed tones, that this trumpeter, Humphrey Lyttelton, was an Old Etonian and Ex-Brigade of Guards Officer, an unlikely and hardly credible combination of parts.

All spoke very highly of his playing and George despatched me to ' The Orange Tree ' one Sunday morning to book Lyttelton for a guest spot at the Hot Club, but he wasn't playing the morning I arrived.

A journalist we knew claimed a close acquaintance with Lyttelton (considering our subsequent knowledge of Lyttelton this was as false a claim as was ever made) and guaranteed his appearance at the Hot Club. We assembled a band to play with him and Humph, a tall, stooping figure with heavy lips and hooded eyes, and wearing a dyed battle-dress, made his first concert appearance in London at the King George's Hall on 8th March 1947. On arrival he swore that his first knowledge of the engagement was from reading a fly-poster. He added that his name had been mis-spelt.

His session was wild and unco-ordinated. It had some of the extreme purists in a rage. Wasn't this the jam session free-for-all the Dixielanders and Hot Club opposed? But Lyttelton stood out as a player with a conception and ability no other British jazz trumpeter had displayed. He was a sensation.

He played an engagement with the Dixielanders at Hawick, in the Scottish lowlands. It was a mystery that the band should have been engaged to play in a place so far remote from any jazz activity, especially as we quoted £75, no small sum for an unknown band in those days.

Reg Rigden, the Dixielanders' first trumpet, was unable to take time off from work and again George sent me to seek out Lyttelton. I went to the Camberwell School of Art where he was studying, waited for him to come out of class and asked him to play the engagement. He didn't appear surprised that it was 332 miles from London, nor did we engage in ungentlemanly haggling about fees, although I vaguely recall that the princely sum of £7 was agreed on.

Rigden subsequently announced he was available, but George directed that the Lyttelton booking should stand. This led to him joining the band and Rigden—we had not got on well—accused me of conspiring to get him out of the band. It was an absurd accusation—George would never have tolerated any interference in the band's affairs.

Humph rehearsed with the band the Sunday morning following our meeting. It was painfully cold. We were in that long, bitter winter of 1946-7 when the fuel crisis was at its worst and my contribution to jazz history that morning was to gather twigs and leaves from the garden to make some sort of fire.

The journey to Hawick was in the aftermath of a snowstorm and took about fourteen hours. On arrival Wally found he had left his clarinet on the train and I spent a couple of sweaty hours tracking it down. It was returned to Hawick and I rushed into the dressing-room five minutes before the show commenced, dramatically brandishing the clarinet.

Attendance was sparse. The locals were disappointed although not particularly on musical grounds. One gentleman was quite

huffy. " We thought you were going to be darkies," he said with
a strong Scottish burr, and that possibly explained how the band
obtained the engagement.

Lyttelton was not only a marvellous trumpeter but an excellent
clarinettist. He was a musical ' natural ' who also had a com-
manding personality and a sharp wit. The appearance of this
physically and musically towering figure from an aristocratic
background in this fundamentally proletarian stir of activity
received considerable publicity. Why not? Neither Humph nor
George sought this kind of attention, but in a class-divided society
such interest was inevitable and the publicity it received, wel-
come. It gave the central figure a certain wry amusement.
It was a unique situation. Old Etonian ex-Guards officers blowing hot jazz trumpets were not thick on the ground and this one
understandably enjoyed being pursued by a wondrous press.

It's certain that there would have been a ' revival ' in Britain
without Webb or Lyttelton but this strange flowering of an alien
culture in a drear-dull London suburb with an upper-crust gent
and a band of factory workers, spearheaded a movement that
spread throughout the country with quite sensational results.

Lyttelton left the Dixielanders in November 1947. It was
inevitable that someone of his stature should lead his own band.
Somewhat peremptorily, he addressed me at ' The Red Barn '
one Monday evening. " This is my swan song, Jim." I had
already received some intimation of this and tried not to show
my concern. Shortly afterwards Wally Fawkes and trombonist
Harry Brown joined Lyttelton. The Dixielanders broke up.

This had been my first taste of the entertainment business. I
feel a certain pride in having played a small part in a unique
crusade, despite the unpleasantness with my adversaries, and
despite the musical hopes never being fully realized. In those
heady days some of us imagined that British jazz, after clearing the first hurdles of apprenticeship, would run in harness
with the American original and fuse with its history and romance.

Considering the social, racial and musical factors it's no
surprise that these aspirations were never realized. They were
no more than the illusions of ardent young romantics. Truth-

fully, I can claim that I wasn't concerned with financial gain. It just didn't occur to me. Had it done, I might have had my eyes open for the prospects that lay around the corner. I got a job with a local sign-writing firm, first selling signs to local shopkeepers and subsequently organizing the various departments. I was the one unskilled employee amongst a dozen or so craftsmen and critically regarded as the guv'nor's man. Not liking this invidious position I left to go and work on the land.

4

HOORAY HENRYS

In November 1949 I returned from agricultural labours as fit
as I'll ever be. I moved into a bed-sitter in Gloucester Place, off
Baker Street, sharing with Ian and Keith Christie. Clarinettist
Ian was short, hunched and waspish, trombonist Keith taller,
gangly, indolent. Both were natural musicians : although only in
their teens, they were playing in Lyttelton's band. They were from
Blackpool and I first met them when they ' sat-in ' with the
Dixielanders. Would jazz historians, I wondered, mention this
significant co-habitation—the influence I had on them, etc. etc.—
along with my steadying Roy Wykes' bass drum in that historic
first private label recording with the Dixielanders at Derby, my
stoking the fire at Lyttelton's first rehearsal with the band at
' The Red Barn ', and my rushing into the dressing-room at
Hawick with Wally Fawkes' clarinet when all seemed lost?

Such stories would surely rank with the anecdote about
American bandleader Eddie Condon's brother Pat leaving a
rehearsal to buy some whisky and next seen some fifteen years
later, and those recollections of the many American jazz musicians who roomed with the legendary cornettist Bix Beiderbecke
and shared his socks. Not that I shared Keith Christie's socks.
These were indisputably his. Stiff with malodorous perspiration
(he was in the R.A.F. at the time and doing a lot of square-
bashing), they were propped up at the end of his bed when he
retired.

It was a small room and had only two beds. I contributed a
collapsible camp bed. Keith, pathologically lazy, could never
muster the strength or will to circumvent or step over it. If it
was in his path, he trod on it and it soon disintegrated. Our rota

of two weeks in proper beds and one in the camp bed also collapsed and we moved into a larger room on the ground floor.

Keith resolutely kept expenditure of energy to the barest minimum. Once Ian left a wet towel on the back of the only armchair and Keith sat in the chair at an acutely uncomfortable position so as not to rest his back on the towel. Removing this to its proper place would have been an unthinkably tiring exercise. Both frequently used the sink as a lavatory bowl and on one occasion this imparted a particular tang to a lettuce I had left soaking.

In the next room lived guitarist Neville Skrimshire, also with Lyttelton, and saxophonist Bruce Turner, playing with Freddy Randall's Band. Every Friday morning the former would awake with a whoop of joy. " Gee, today's *Melody Maker* day !" The latter, always raffishly attired in a silk dressing-gown, had assignations with a variety of ladies that often resulted in harsh words, for which we avidly listened.

The rest of the occupants loathed us, and we fought a running battle with a haughty female on the first floor who abhorred jazz and claimed she was a classical impresario, her business, we observed, being conducted from the coin-box telephone in the hallway just outside of our room. We had an archetypal Irish landlady, Mrs Mitchell, who frequently castigated us. Rightly so, for we used to play records at full volume well after the permitted hour and were often noisily drunk, but she was a good-hearted lady and her outbursts of fury would dissolve into throaty chuckles.

Exasperated by the Christies' incredible untidiness and the sock-befouled atmosphere, I jumped at the chance of occupying a small room that had become vacant at the end of the hall.

When Mrs Mitchell was doing her chores and muttering critically about " them Christies ", I would wholeheartedly agree with her. " A *dreadful* pair, Mrs Mitchell," I would say and if I played records late at night I blamed it on the Christies. My assiduous cultivation of the landlady's goodwill was shattered one embarrassing morning. All the ' guests ' were supposed to leave by eleven o'clock at night, a regulation consistently if surreptitiously ignored. I was in bed with my girlfriend and had left the door unlocked. Hearing the latch turn I leapt up to push the door back. By the time I had sprung to the bottom of the bed, Mrs Mitchell had opened the door and she stood transfixed at the spectacle of me naked and erect, in both senses, in a stance not unlike Eros, without the bow and wings and with an expression more strained than seraphic.

I landed a job with Bert and Stan Wilcox editing their just-launched *Jazz Illustrated*, a monthly photo-magazine. At the end of the 'forties the brothers Wilcox, with no previous jazz associations, had suddenly emerged as the country's foremost jazz promoters, running the London Jazz Club at Windmill Street, featuring the Lyttelton Band and promoting concerts. I was engaged on rather slender credentials, having written nothing more than some ' satirical ' pieces in their club news-letter under the name of ' Odbot '.

Jazz Illustrated was a lush production compared with the small home-produced magazines being published at the time. I received eight pounds a week for my important and responsible position as editor and produced my first issue from a corner of a small desk in a tiny room at the back of the Wilcox radio shop in St John's Wood High Street, standing up. There was no room for the editor's desk and chair.

The end product showed there was something amiss in the production line, not to mention the journalistic shortcomings of its editor. Mistakes, I'm sorry to say, were thick between the covers. In one issue I apologized for previous errors and claimed that " we " had been through the current issue with a fine tooth comb to eliminate the errors. I jocularly invited " pedants " to get cracking and prove me wrong.

A super-pedant obliged. He sent me a detailed list of mistakes divided into five columns listing the page, the column, the paragraph, the line, the error and the correction. Fifty-two in all: split infinitives, mis-spellings, typographical inconsistencies, omitted hyphens, inversions and many more in a shattering compilation.

I checked just in case he was wrong. He was, but only because he had overlooked two mistakes. I wrote thanking him for his scrutiny, congratulated him on his scholarship but, apropos the errors he had overlooked, I suggested he be more careful next time. It was a feeble riposte and there was no next time. The magazine folded. It was losing too much money.

When writing this book I braced myself and looked through copies of *Jazz Illustrated*. I shuddered occasionally but, withal, it wasn't too bad an attempt at something new in jazz journalism and Humphrey Lyttelton's cartoons of famous jazzmen are gems.

The Wilcoxes had started a band agency run by Les Perrin. Perrin had a mass of exploding ideas and was constantly flying off at different tangents, sometimes, it seemed, simultaneously. He also handled publicity for the Wilcoxes' artistes and promotions. After the collapse of *Jazz Illustrated*, the Wilcoxes decided that Les should stick to publicity and that I should handle the agency side. I honestly can't recall a single word of discussion that led to this fateful step. Maybe, in the light of my subsequent experiences as an agent/booker, this memory blank has Freudian significance. Nor can I recall how much I was paid for the job. I have a vague idea it was the same salary I received during my short-lived grandeur as editor of a glossy magazine.

I was soon to discover there was no grandeur in being a band booker.

My first booking responsibilities were two ' modern ' jazz bands —the Johnny Dankworth Seven and Kenny Graham's Afro-Cubists, the leaders both brilliant arrangers and fine musicians, Johnny on clarinet and alto saxophone and Kenny on tenor saxophone. Their music was inspired by the then new ' Be-bop ' school of American jazzmen, trumpeter Dizzy Gillespie, alto-saxophonist Charlie Parker and pianist Theolonius Monk. Both bands had only a limited appeal, and the struggle to find them work quickly gave me an insight into the mechanics and harsh realities of band-booking. It is, in any case, a job that can only be picked up by day-to-day experience.

Graham's band was particularly difficult to sell. Kenny would put his head round my office door (the Wilcoxes had moved to Earlham Street, off Cambridge Circus) and dolefully enquire if there was any work. Les Perrin (who has since become the most famous and respected of P.R.O.s, with a dazzling list of famous clients) worked hard on publicity (" Don't Be A Square,

Be An Afro-Cubist ") but I quickly discovered that publicity alone never sold bands.

Dankworth's band was easier to book. It had a more ' commercial' sound and Johnny had been top of the *Melody Maker* polls as arranger, alto-saxophonist and musician of the year. Kenny, a gruff, genuine person, was slightly resentful that he wasn't getting as much work as Johnny and thought favouritism the reason. This wasn't the case. An agent/booker would sooner earn commission from two bands than from just one, let alone saving himself the embarrassment of facing the workless band-leader day by day.

Kenny's band was musically excellent but its lack of drawing power taught me that the public are not wholly interested in good musicianship. The rapport between artiste and audience is often an intangible magnetism or an element of showmanship quite separate from musical ability.

Dankworth's Seven, although sincerely dedicated to Be-bop (and none more than its trombonist, one Eddie Harvey, whose reprehensible deviationism in the Webb days was bearing fruit in this band), compromised by playing current hits. They had a marvellous husky-voiced singer with a remarkable range. Her name was Cleo Laine, since internationally famous.

Johnny was a nice person but he had a rather annoying penchant for sitting on my desk and cracking peanuts over my date sheets. Recently he was awarded an O.B.E. and now, mostly writing formal music, prefers to be known as John Dankworth.

In the late 'forties and early 'fifties, the schism between the traditionalists and modernists was extremely pronounced. From entrenched positions, the protagonists belted abuse at each other, the traditionalists by far the more bigoted of the protagonists and given to stern moral postures. We knew our water-tight artistic compartments in those days!

Now that I was acutely involved in the economics of jazz, my private convictions were subjugated, although I was probably certifiably schizoid in my determined pursuit of bookings for modernists whilst still a passionate traditionalist.

Bert, the elder of the Wilcoxes, was an amiable and self-effacing man but the architect of the company's more bizarre schemes : he was out to build an empire in the shortest possible time.

Whilst *Jazz Illustrated* was still being published, he signed the Vic Lewis Concert Orchestra for a nation-wide tour, under the heading " Music For Moderns ". The grandiose nomenclature of the orchestra and the fancy title of the show had me seeking refuge behind the nearest pile of unsold *Illustrated*s that lay about the office, but Bert blithely took them at a large salary and with the additional cost of organizing the concerts. My objections to " Music For Moderns " were not entirely musical. I didn't see it as a commercial proposition and indeed it proved to be a highly expensive failure and deservedly so. It was no more than a pretentious farrago of half-baked classicism with bits of solo Be-bop thrown in, the whole flamboyantly ' conducted ' by the leader. It was in direct imitation of American bandleader Stan Kenton who started this kind of confection but with a band that had a lot more verve and talent than Lewis could muster.

Later, when I was running the agency, one of Bert's more inexplicable actions was to sign an Olde Tyme Orchestra, an ensemble quite out of keeping with the image of the office. As a result I had yet another, although older, face peering round my office door and the owner, a man called Leon Smallbone, anxiously enquired if there was any work for his Olde Tyme Orchestra. He would insist on playing me test pressings of waltzes, valetas, glides and two-steps his orchestra had recorded. Mr Smallbone came to see me nearly every day, but I failed to obtain a single engagement for his orchestra. There was a date sheet on my desk that required a lot more urgent attention.

Bert had signed Graeme Bell's Australian Jazz Band for a nine months' tour of this country at a guaranteed salary plus fares from Australia and travelling expenses in this country.

The Bell band had appeared at the Hot Club of London in 1947, after barnstorming Czechoslovakia, a courageous adventure. They stayed in England with great success pioneering what was then the almost heretical idea of dancing to jazz. Prior to then, audiences had listened to the music with heads nodding metronomically, the males with pipes firmly clenched in hand or teeth. There was a lot of pipe smoking amongst jazz buffs in

those days. The pipe emphasized the seriousness of our concentration on the intricacies of the inner rhythms and the
contrapuntal interplay. Happily, the Bell band altered all this.
They urged people to dance and promoted a lively and relaxed
atmosphere and thereby drew a larger audience to jazz.

On their return to this country they faced strong competition
from British bands that had improved considerably since their first
visit, and they had, anyway, lost a lot of their sparkle. Booking
them sufficiently lucrative engagements to cover costs and perhaps
recoup some of the travel costs was difficult. Profit was a dream
that curled from my much-puffed pipe. Not that the Australians
admitted any failings. There was more than a touch of normal
antipodean cockiness about them and Graeme was given to
making patronizing remarks about British bands.

I got on well with their manager, Ernest 'Mel' Langdon, a
bluff, resilient character and happily for me, realistic and open
about the band's earning capacity. He was fond of a drink and
spoke an initially bewildering ' strine ' : " I'm off to a sneak go
[an obscure bar] to get a taste [a drink] and see this Sheila
[girl]." He used such beguiling phrases as " old as God's dog "
and, referring to tight-fisted musicians, " They've got an impedi-
ment in their reach," and if two hard cases arrived at the bar
simultaneously there would be a " battle of the giants " and we
were witness to many a titanic struggle amongst the giants in the
Bell band.

Mel and I used to have a few drinks after office hours and
once visiting the London Jazz Club, watched with mounting
amusement the dancing dervish antics of the Guardees and their
debutante ladies who attended only when Humphrey Lyttelton's
Band was appearing. Their movements on the floor were, without
exception, wild, totally unrhythmic and it was physically dangerous to be in proximity when they were in full thrash. A description hit me as we gaped at the spectacle. I had then recently
read a selection of Damon Runyon stories. In one of them,
" Tight Shoes ", there was a rich layabout called Calvin Colby.
Runyon described him as " Strictly a Hooray Henry "*. Of

* Runyon's actual term was " Hurrah Henry ", which I misread as " Hooray
Henry ", pronounced it as such and the phrase stuck.

course! These galumphing Guardees were Hooray Henrys! I
made the reference, got an amused reaction and "Hooray
Henry" entered jazz terminology and, as with terminology from
other minority groups, has since passed into wider usage.

My initiation into the rites of booking bands in the Wilcox
Organization soon made me realize that the popular conception
of an agent as a corpulent shark automatically better off by
ten per cent of the negotiated fee every time he picked up the
telephone was one big myth, and there were alarming pitfalls.

Les Perrin was a great help to me in this initiation period. He
warned me about the agent's bug-bear—barring clauses—those
stipulations in the contract that preclude an artiste or band
appearing in an area within a time and distance bar of the date
of the engagement. His advice didn't always stick and I overlooked many a barring clause, resulting in many disputes.

Les was a likeable, warm-hearted person but could be
extremely infuriating. He had a meandering, interpolative mode
of address and it took him an inordinate time to make a simple
observation. We had an argument that resulted in a flurry of
fists, sheaves of paper billowing into the air and the telephone
cord strung round my neck. The difference of opinion was over
the release of a news story that the Dankworth band was going
to refuse all B.B.C. "Jazz Club" engagements. They had made
the compromise necessary for survival and didn't wish to be
typed purely as a jazz band and possibly deter ballroom promoters from booking them. This was the classic dilemma that
had faced many American bands led and manned by jazzmen
and here it was on my doorstep. I don't recall my objections to
the story being released. I think I was about to make a B.B.C.
Jazz Club booking when Les intervened. Whatever, a comic
scuffle ensued. Undoubtedly, I was at fault. I was in a state of
considerable nervous tension—I had yet to take the hurly-burly
nature of a booker's life into my stride—and the office at the
time had the appearance of Waterloo station in the rush
hour.

Conveniently situated in the West End, it had become a
meeting place for a mixed assortment of people, some connected
with the business, some not.

Mr Smallbone had probably been in to play me a Boston
Two-Step; maybe I had overlooked a barring clause; the Bell
Band were undoubtedly complaining about the kind of engagements I had managed to squeeze from a business coldly indifferent to their talents; Kenny Graham's Band was teetering on the
edge of the breadline.

Conditions at Earlham Street were further complicated by
Bert launching out as a theatre impresario. His first, and only,
venture in this hazardous area of show business was a production
called " Non-Stop Hollywood " and Bert had found a backer
in bandleader Mick Mulligan. " Non-Stop Hollywood " came
to an abrupt halt after only two weeks and all Mick Mulligan
got for his investment of £2,000 was one of the chorus girls
on the opening night, surely the most expensive night of passion
in the whole history of show-biz.

Prior to the show opening a procession of comedians, jugglers,
impersonators and chorus girls were interviewed in my office,
there being no other space available. The producer of the show
had the girls show him their knees, these joints being well covered
when the girls arrived by the voluminous ' New Look ' skirts
of the time. With this succession of titillating flashes going on
before my compulsive gaze, it was difficult to concentrate on the
affairs of the Seven, the Afro-Cubists, the Australians and Mr
Smallbone. Les and I went for a drink in the pub next door
almost immediately after our scuffle and Dankworth's decision
made the headlines in the next issue of the *Melody Maker*. It
also made Les's point but, a month or so later, the Dankworth
band returned to B.B.C. " Jazz Club " as if nothing had
happened.

Disasters struck the Wilcox office. After the failure of " Music
For Moderns " and " Non-Stop Hollywood ", there were further
blows. The Dankworth band signed to another agency and
Humph's management, not slow to notice the marked disparity
between the money Humph was getting at the packed London
Jazz Club, now at 100 Oxford Street, and the money Vic Lewis
was receiving for playing to poor houses, claimed an increase.
It was refused and the association between the Wilcoxes and
Lyttelton ceased.

On the band's final night at the club, Stan Wilcox twice announced there had been differences between themselves, the employers and Lyttelton, the employee, and the association was to close as a result. Lyttelton's expression as he was referred to as an ' employee ' the second time time was worth seeing. In my mind's eye I can still see it. Rebel he may have been but his class conditioning was immutable and his impassivity cracked. Not much, but enough to show.

The empire that had suddenly flourished, collapsed with even greater speed. I felt very sorry for Bert, but he had only his delusions of grandeur to blame for the catastrophes. It was a classic example of healthy resources wasted on wild-cat projects. It should have been a salutary lesson to me. It wasn't. Later I made the same sort of mistakes.

I left the Wilcoxes and went into partnership with Mel Langdon, representing the Bell band and Kenny Baker's Band. Kenny had consistently been in the popularity polls as Britain's No. 1 trumpet player with Britain's top swing band, Ted Heath's. It was another lesson to me. To make a name with a particular band doesn't necessarily ensure success at the box office with your own. Kenny was a nice person and a superbly skilled player but his band was far too ' modern ' to be a success.

Mel and I operated from a small room in the Lyttelton office rented to us at a nominal sum. It was difficult to make our venture pay its way. The maximum we could obtain for the Bell band was £60 and had to take jobs as low as £30 to make up the weekly gross. If we managed to accrue a weekly total of £200 we were lucky and out of this figure we had to pay the band, ourselves and our overheads.

To boost our income we organized our own promotions. One was at the Town Hall, Aylesbury, with the Bell band. We arrived at 6.30 p.m., a time of the evening we didn't expect to see any customers but we sniffed portending disaster. Mel, part consciously, had a film-style manner redolent of the 'thirties and 'forties. I think he saw himself as a genial cynic breezily facing adversity after the fashion of Bruce Cabot or Lee Tracy, actors who graced many a ' B ' picture at the pre-war Odeons. He and I stood outside the portals of this Victorian Town Hall and looked around. " I smell a blue duck," he said, grinning.

Kenny Graham (tenor), Johnny Dankworth (alto, clarinet), un-identified trumpeter; *Behind:* Carlo Krahmer (drums), Russ Allen (bass). *(Photo: P. D. Lord)*

London Jazz Club, 100 Oxford St, London W.1. November 1949
(Photo: Radio Times Hulton)

Riverboat Shuffle *(Photo : Radto Times Hulton)*

London Jazz Club, November 1949. *Left to right:* Stan Wilcox, Humphrey Lyttelton, Wally Fawkes, Ian Christie and Keith Christie
(Photo : Radio Times Hulton)

Which is exactly what it turned out to be. Or, in plain English, a dreadful flop. About a dozen people paid to enter. The atmosphere was utterly depressing and Langdon suggested we found a sneak go and had a taste although he was doubtful there would be any Sheilas available in a one-horse town like Aylesbury, Bucks.

We got by—just. The band cut their salaries and some of their wives reluctantly found jobs, although not without tart reference to the inadequacy of the band's booker.

When the band returned to Australia Graeme Bell's parting shot, quoted in the *Melody Maker*, was that " If British bands stuck at it and rehearsed they should improve." The Australians brought a breezy humour, fresh approach and a wide repertoire to jazz presentation, but modesty was not one of their shining attributes, and their leader was patently unaware of the word.

5

THE M.U., THE M.O.L. AND MR MORLEY

When the Bell band returned to Australia in 1951, I joined forces with Lyn Dutton, he managing and booking the Lyttelton band and I booking the Mick Mulligan, Chris Barber and Crane River bands. Representation of Chris was almost a total failure. He was a likeable young man and, unlike most revivalists had studied music—at the Guildhall School of Music—but initially he was hopeless at leading a band. Later, he took over leadership of another band and quickly rocketed to fame although, unfortunately, not signed to me.

The association with Lyn was pleasant, but short-lived. Even though more and more promoters were taking jazz bands the agency wasn't paying its way. Some promoters were presenting mammoth concerts featuring up to fifteen bands at a time, each band naturally playing their rabble rousers in the short time they were allocated. There was a complete absence of presentation. It was generally agreed that these concerts were harmful to jazz and I submitted to Ed. W. Jones, a respected promoter, the idea of a concert with only a few bands playing in different styles to illustrate various phases of jazz history to be presented with a linking commentary. Jones accepted the idea.

I wrote a simple script and engaged an ex-U.S. Army Radio announcer to be the unseen commentator from one side of the stage and myself at the other. It was, at least, an attempt at production and the programme was well balanced. Called *The Story of Jazz* it was staged at the old Trocadero, Elephant and Castle, in South London.

The programme was a complete success, with both houses well attended and received enthusiastic press notices. One critic

wrote I was the " Answer Man " to the problem of staging jazz
concerts but the market had been thoroughly soaked with the
boring mammoth concert bringing about a sharp decline in jazz
concerts generally.

In 1950 Lyn Dutton booked the legendary New Orleans
blues singer and guitarist Lonnie Johnson for a tour of Britain,
to be accompanied by British bands. The booking was made
with the National Federation of Jazz Organizations, a non-
profit making body formed by enthusiasts to promote jazz generally. They obtained work permits for Johnson's visit from the
Ministry of Labour but the British Musicians Union goose-
stepped in and strictly forbade the bands from appearing with
him, as their permission had not been sought.

Since the mid 'thirties, the Musicians Union had been successful in preventing American bands from appearing in the U.K.
on the grounds that their entry would rob British musicians of
work. The case was feasible with regard to formal *dance* bands
but they could not, or would not, accept that jazz musicians
were a special case.

From 1933 jazz enthusiasts had been denied the pleasure of
hearing in the flesh the players they knew on record and in 1950
in the full surge of revivalism there were vehement objections
from the jazz fraternity to the M.U.'s obduracy. The M.U.'s
attitude in the Johnson case was particularly mystifying as
British bands had been booked to appear with him and surely
they couldn't have objected to him putting blues singers out of
work since we didn't have any?

Moreover, the M.U. executive was dominated by individuals
with a political hatred of America. My belief is that had there
been any Russian jazz musicians they would have been over here
in droves, with the M.U.'s fervent blessing.

The M.U.'s directive came too late for Johnson's contract to
be cancelled and the N.F.J.O. had extensively advertised his
appearance at the Festival Hall, this apart from their contract
with Lyn Dutton. As the bands were forbidden to appear, other
arrangements had to be made. Marie Bryant, a well-known
Harlem cabaret performer who had appeared in the classic
film short *Jammin' The Blues* was in the country, and was booked

to partner Lonnie. The tour was not a great success, partly due to Johnson singing treacly songs instead of the blues, but partly because the traditional style bands didn't appear. This was significant. Owing to the ban on American jazz musicians, the local product was fast becoming accepted over the American original, a situation that was to develop during the ensuing ' trad ' boom.

I travelled part of the tour. Johnson, then sixty years of age and confused by the politics surrounding his visit, had another unexpected cross to bear—jazz record collectors. He had played guitar on record with Duke Ellington and Louis Armstrong and was besieged by ardent discophiles who pummelled him with questions about the past (I was one of them) and plied him with drinks he didn't want (not by me). One of his questioners, a jazz ' authority ' forcibly removed him from my presence in an attempt to whisk him away to the suburbs, ply him with more drink and badger him with more questions. I had to collect Lonnie from his hotel the following morning and board a train to Liverpool and refused to let him go. To Lonnie's distress there was a fierce argument between this ' authority ' and myself but I won the day. When I called for Johnson the following day he was relatively fresh. He most certainly would have been otherwise had he been spirited away and his memory thoroughly, exhaustingly ransacked.

Lena Horne was appearing at the Liverpool Empire and invited Lonnie to visit her after he had finished his show. I honestly can't recall if I was invited—I think I was—but three members of the Merseysippi Jazz Band (who had been booked to appear with Lonnie until the M.U. decreed otherwise) came along at my invitation and four utter strangers presented themselves at Miss Horne's apartment. It was an awful bit of cheek on my part but we were cordially greeted by her husband and musical director, Lennie Hayton.

Hayton had played on records with cornettist Bix Beiderbecke and he came in for some lengthy questioning about Bix and these recordings. He took the eager questioning in good humour but dryly remarked that as we appeared to know more about those records than he did himself, perhaps we could leave it at that.

Lena Horne entered the room. She had a striking beauty, with eyes of quite hypnotic luminosity. She looked so gorgeous we were spellbound and practically speechless. We forgot about Bix Beiderbecke. She soon excused herself but not before Lonnie had respectfully addressed her as " Missie Horne ". Lonnie, a coloured man born in New Orleans before the turn of the century, grew up at a time when race barriers were very marked. Lena Horne was an international star, lighter skinned and, being much younger, had pronounced and well-publicized views on racial inequality. The difference between these two of the same race, although neither pure negro, was quite striking and crystallized in Lonnie's deferential reference.

The unfortunate story of Lonnie's tour had a regrettable finale. The Festival Hall concert was a fiasco because of the enforced changes in the programme and poor programme planning but, to their credit, a few musicians defied the Union and appeared, Lonnie Donegan, George Webb and George Melly amongst them.

True it had been remiss of the N.F.J.O. not to have sought the permission of the Union—it was known they were a powerful body—but this didn't excuse the latter's iron-fisted attitude, especially as Ministry of Labour permits had been granted. The Union issued a statement :

" The Union object to the appearance of foreign musicians unless under arrangements approved by the Union for the two jazz concerts [one was a ' modern ' jazz concert]. Arrangements were made without consultation with the Union by the N.F.J.O. who first wrote to the Union asking for consideration of the ' ban ' [the M.U.'s quote marks] only on 25th June, received on the 26th. The first concert was held on the 28th.

" The Ministry of Labour decided in April that the foreign musicians could perform but merely informed the Union of the decision without any prior consultation, despite the fact that such consultation is the usual practice.

" We are not willing to be told by the Ministry; we should have been consulted by them and the N.F.J.O. before the bookings were made. The N.F.J.O. admitted that this should have been done by expressing ' deepest regret ' on 25th June, but it was too late then.

" Relations with other countries are not involved in this case.

We will discuss any scheme to regulate foreign bookings but will not be ignored by the N.F.J.O. until a few days before the concert."

What colossal arrogance! The " usual practices " they referred to were their customary bludgeoning of the Ministry to accept their restrictive practices, the Ministry of Labour having no statutory obligation to accept instructions from the Musicians Union, or indeed any other Union or body, excepting the Home Office and then primarily in the case of undesirable aliens.

Further, as the N.F.J.O. had booked the Festival Hall and the support programme what else could they do but eat humble pie by " expressing regrets " in the hope of mollifying these blinkered fossils at Sicilian Avenue, Holborn, where the M.U. had their headquarters? The N.F.J.O. was an organization making an attempt to bring revered jazzmen and blues singers into the country, many of them in their middle years and soon to pass on. Their aims were entirely laudable. The M.U.'s opposition to this was utterly stupid.

Later the Musicians Union disciplined the musicians who defied the ban and those who obeyed the ban went without the work they could have had if the ban had not been imposed. An *Alice in Wonderland* situation.

I organized a broad-based platform of musicians and journalists to speak their minds against the M.U.'s undue influence. My aim was not financial gain. I didn't have enough capital to launch any of these jazzmen in this country but I was convinced that limited entry of these players would be good for the jazz business generally and even if I, and others like me, were wrong what right had a gaggle of old theatre pit musicians to stand in the way of these unique artistes appearing in this country for the pleasure of thousands who should have had the right to decide for themselves who they should listen to, and when?

I booked the Caxton Hall for the meeting and the following agreed to speak. Ernest Borneman (author, anthropologist, film maker, jazz critic of considerable scholarship), Pat Brand (editor of the *Melody Maker*), Bob Farnon (composer and orchestra leader), Humphrey Lyttelton, Steve Race (musician and journalist) and Ray Sonin (editor of the *Musical Express*).

With respected names like these, the meeting was not a frivolous or hot-headed exercise. I had a difficult task in persuading the editors of the rival papers to appear on the same platform, to get each to mention the other in their respective papers, something neither had ever done before. It was my one and only achievement. The meeting didn't take place. Although it was made clear in prior announcements that the meeting was not in any way an anti-Union demonstration, nor were we asking for uncontrolled entry of foreign musicians, I received a call from Steve Race a few days before the meeting advising me that he couldn't appear as the Union had warned him that any member appearing on that platform would be severely disciplined. Race told me he would have to advise Bob Farnon not to speak. The Union claimed that if members wanted to alter Union policy in any way, the right and proper place was at Union meetings, and any resolutions would be passed to the executive in due course.

This left Humphrey Lyttelton as the only musician on the platform and I couldn't reasonably ask him to stand alone. Without musicians on the platform, the M.U. could allege that I was acting for purely business reasons (being an agent assuredly made me a wicked capitalist in their eyes), that the newspapers were in it for the publicity and that the musicians whose interests were being put at risk, were absent.

It was essential that there be a broad-based platform. I had to abandon the meeting, pay for the hire of the hall and the cost of the printing. I was stymied by a narrow-minded, myopic bunch of reactionaries. Further, I was now in bad odour with the Union. I was informed by friendly musicians who attended a meeting of the Central London Branch that when my name came up there were grunts of disapproval and heads nodded in agreement that I was an enemy of the Union.

Illogical thinking. As an agent I would benefit from musicians' increased earnings and protection of their interests. I did manage to speak to one high official, Harry Francis. It was a friendly meeting and he was plainly bewildered. He said, " You know, Jim, I can't understand what all the fuss is about. Why do you want to bring Louis Armstrong in when you can hear Kenny Baker? You can't tell me there's a finer trumpet player in the world than Kenny." It was a query and an opinion that brought me to my knees. We were in different worlds, speaking a different language, and I'm at a loss for a parallel.

In November 1949 the great Creole soprano saxophonist and clarinettist, Sidney Bechet, appeared, illegally, at the Winter Garden Theatre, London. Ostensibly the occasion was a concert featuring Humphrey Lyttelton and his Band, organized by the Wilcox brothers, but the word was spread through the jazz bush telegraph that Bechet would also be appearing and the 1,800-capacity hall was fully packed with a crowd that throbbed in anticipation of a great event.

Critic Rex Harris compered the show. He read out a critique of Bechet's playing written, amazingly, not in a current jazz magazine, nor even in the 'thirties when discoveries were being made by the dozen, but in *1919*, and even more astonishing, the author was the famous Swiss conductor, Ernest Ansermet. This critique makes Ansermet the first ever jazz ' critic ' to commit his views to print, thirty years before this memorable night.

"There is in the Southern Syncopated Orchestra an extraordinary clarinet virtuoso who, it seems, is the first in his race to have composed perfectly composed blues on the clarinet. I've heard two of them which he elaborated at great length. They are admirable equally for the richness of their invention, their force of accent, their daring novelty and unexpected turns. Their form is gripping, abrupt, harsh with a brusque and pitiless ending like that of Bach's Second Brandenburg Concerto. I wish to set down the name of this artiste of genius—it is Sidney Bechet—who can say nothing of his art except that it follows his ' own way '—and then one considers that perhaps his is the way we will swing down the road of the future!"

This was incredible foresight from a ' classical ' musician of world renown. It was not until nearly twenty years later that the jazz cognoscenti ' discovered ' Sidney Bechet.

After reading the tribute Harris indicated a box above the left-hand side of the stage and the spotlight shone on Sidney Bechet, jazzman supreme. At Harris's invitation he joined Humph's band and the crowd were rapturous with delight. Here, at last, was a genius of jazz playing before our very eyes, a historic event that the Musicians Union and the Ministry of

Labour would have stopped had they known of it—hence the unusual form of advertising to thwart their inevitable interference.

Shortly afterwards different promoters, Bix Curtis and Tony Hughes, brought in the great American negro saxophonist, Coleman Hawkins, to play at the Cambridge Theatre. The circumstances were similar, except that a great deal of publicity surrounded the appearance of Hawkins.

Curtis, Hughes and Wilcox were individually and collectively summoned. Admittedly they had promoted illegal performances—and there's a crime! Genius the like of which the world will never know again actually playing before British audiences. Criminal indeed!

All three stood trial, but Bert was also charged with aiding and abetting the illegal entry of Hawkins, in which he definitely had no part. The charges against them on separate counts were inevitable. The Ministry of Labour had previously turned down applications for work permits, undoubtedly under pressure from the Musicians Union. The Ministry of Labour relied heavily on the recommendations of 'experts' in the industrial field regarding labour permits generally and in this sphere of entertainment the Musicians Union were the 'experts'. The Ministry's quite proper desire not to admit workers that could engender industrial strife had been extended to the exclusion of American jazz musicians on the M.U.'s expert advice that these would put British musicians out of work. It was a false postulate. But civil servants at the Ministry were unaware of this. It could reasonably be said that these allegedly non-political gentlemen were no more 'hep'—to use jazz slang—to the real situation than the bigoted Union officials of extreme left-wing allegiance who dominated the Union's policy.

It was a unique case. The trial lasted several days and many witnesses, including Rex Harris and Humphrey Lyttelton, were called to give evidence. In his book *I Play As I Please* (McGibbon, Kee & Pan Books) Humph claims that he was prepared to play with Bechet even at the risk of imprisonment, yet was allusively critical of Bert's part in the affair and of the musical press that supported his actions—an odd contradiction.

The offenders were heavily fined, but the cost to the country to bring to trial three men whose crime was to present two great artistes of supreme talent must have run into thousands of pounds. Indeed the law was an ass! As was a certain judge. Bert Wilcox appealed against the palpably unjust fine for aiding and abetting the illegal entry of Hawkins and the hearing touched on the bizarre.

The Appeal Judge, Lord Goddard, used unbelievably convoluted terminology in his summing-up. Jazz people had long been used to their music being misrepresented and maligned by those who enforce and interpret the law; long accustomed to witticisms from the bench ("And what, pray, is a saxophone, exactly?") but Lord Goddard's inexactitudes were beyond belief.

The noble Lord said, "Hawkins, who is a celebrated professor of the *trumpet* [my italics] performed on this instrument as well as the saxophone." He accused Bert of "not standing up in the name of the musicians of England to protest that Hawkins ought not to be playing and competing with them and taking the bread out of their mouths *and the wind out of their instruments*." [My italics].

"It is not known whether he [Wilcox] actively applauded the performance but he wrote a most laudatory description, fully illustrated, in his magazine *Jazz Illustrated*. Wilcox's presence was not accidental. He went there for the purpose of getting copy for his magazine knowing it was illegal for this man [Hawkins] to play. If he had booed or if he had been a member of the *claque* [again my italics] that had gone to drown the saxophone [not the trumpet?] he might not have been held for aiding and abetting but in this case he was there for approving and encouraging what was done and taking advantage of it."

The mind boggles even to write this exactly as it was reported. Could there have been a summing-up as muddled, meaningless and preposterously inept as this in the whole of legal history? We all know that judges are notorious for their little jokes but this aspect of the appeal became quite farcical.

In complaining about Wilcox, a magazine proprietor, reporting an event that was illegal, was he was suggesting a dangerous precedent? Should, then, newspapers not report crimes? As for

Bert booing a distinguished soloist or joining a claque (non-existent) to drown the saxophone . . .

Apart from Wilcox's right to attend a public concert, what were certain British musicians present thinking as they watched French musicians accompanying Hawkins when, but for the M.U.'s ban, they could have had the honour and the financial reward? It was hardly Hawkins or Wilcox who were taking the bread out of their mouths (or the wind out of their instruments, whatever that meant). It was the stupid and stubborn Musicians Union putting pressure on the Ministry of Labour to enforce a law designed to keep out prostitutes, criminals and unwanted foreign labour. The fundamental stupidity of the charge (irrespective of the legalities), the intransigence of the Musicians Union, the meek acceptance of their strictures by the Ministry of Labour, the miscarriage of justice and Goddard's summing-up had all the elements of a comic opera.

Bert Wilcox undoubtedly had hopes of financial gain from his technically illegal act of presenting Sidney Bechet but he deserved the thanks of all jazz enthusiasts for bringing to a head the absurdity of the ban. Shortly afterwards many pressures were brought to bear on the Musicians Union and soon a more rational situation obtained, but not before many great jazz musicians of the old school had died or gone into decline.

Thanks to those curmudgeons with closed minds at Sicilian Avenue, a whole generation had been denied seeing a unique minstrelsy, the like of which will not be known again.

During my time with Lyn Dutton I tried to interest Mecca Ballrooms in employing jazz bands. I was granted an interview with Mr Eric Morley, now Managing Director of Mecca and famous for his sponsorship of the edifying Miss World contests. I told him about the jazz revival making its impact in ballrooms throughout the country and proposed that our office book jazz bands for his ballrooms. Mr Morley put his feet up on his desk, waved a silver pencil before his nose and said, " Mr Godbolt, I am a man of taste. I play several musical instruments and consider jazz to be an abomination. As long as *I* have anything to do with Mecca Ballrooms no jazz will be played in our halls. Good *day*, Mr Godbolt."

A few years later when the traditional jazz boom was relatively big business, I was baulked in my attempt to book Acker Bilk's Band, the country's biggest attraction at the time, to play Edinburgh for a client of mine, Duncan McKinnon, and before that Duncan had been the first to book Acker in Scotland.

How was I baulked? By a more lucrative offer from another organization with a ballroom in Edinburgh—Mecca Ballrooms, in fact—and Acker's booking came directly through the office in that organization administered by that multi-instrumentalist of taste and organizer of the Miss World Contests, Mr Eric Morley.

6

MICK MULLIGAN AND BERT AMBROSE

By 1952 I was in business on my own account working in a tiny dungeon in a back street off Tottenham Court Road. Financially I was in a bad way. Eddie Harvey offered me a loan and Duncan McKinnon, operating a chain of dance halls in the Scottish lowlands, gave me sole booking of London-based bands into his venues. I was representing Mick Mulligan and his Band, featuring singer George Melly. This was a traditional-style jazz band but Mick had dispensed with the plonking banjo then common in similar bands. I was extremely grateful to Eddie for the loan, and to Duncan for his business, but there were times when I had grave misgivings about the association with Mick, although this lasted for ten years, right up to the time he disbanded.

Our initial meetings were hardly cordial and when he surprisingly asked me to become his agent I mockingly refused. We met again, he repeated the offer and shook hands on a verbal agreement that I was to represent his band. It was an odd start to a relationship that was constantly stormy and, for me, frequently bordered on the traumatic.

Mick was a wild man; inconstant, highly exasperating but, at his best, very funny and extremely likeable. His agent was something of a querulous paranoiac although not, I like to think, without humour. It was a combination of parts alternately harmonious and combustible. Mick had the most winning ways and knew it, but they didn't always mollify me and considering the pitch and frequency of our battles it surprised me that he didn't sign with another agent.

Whether he would have been any better off had he signed

elsewhere is now purely conjectural, but he could have easily determined this by dispensing with my services.

Perhaps he didn't change offices out of 'loyalty', an attribute Mick highly praised and demanded in others—although in his case it usually meant his agent and personnel going along with his highly idiosyncratic behaviour. I didn't and there were fierce rows. He was a good friend ('loyal' he'd say) when at one stage of my career I was without an office and he gave me the use of his flat and telephone. Later, at another crucial stage, I told him I was ceasing business altogether and he was most insistent that I didn't, and helped me financially. Working from his flat in Lisle Street, near Soho, was an inconvenience to him and beset with dangers for me. I accompanied him to nearby pubs more often than was good for my health, my pocket, or, such as it was, my business. Had Mick sacked me, then I might have left the business for good. On the other hand, had I spent less time with this hell-raiser and his fellow ravers, I might have taken the matter of being in business more seriously. Not a world-shattering consideration, but I give it the occasional thought.

Intermingled with the arguments there were some hilarious moments. We had a lot of laughter together and although utterly diametrical in character had a close affinity. The bad moments were quite upsetting, for Mick could be unpleasantly abusive when drunk, and something of a bully if he thought anyone beholden to him. When I retaliated, he would often turn on the hurt-surprised tone and/or expression, protest that I had misunderstood him and suggest, "You had better come and have a drink, cock," an invitation which, if accepted, inevitably resulted in my collapsing in a drunken heap several hours later, often with his ferocious, evil-smelling bull terrier, Twist, as a bed-mate.

"Just *one* then, cock!" was his cry should the invitation be refused, an entreaty I learned to regard with apprehension. There was no such thing as 'just one' with Mick. I can't possibly recall the number of times I got drunk with him and the effect these marathons had on my health in general and my liver in particular, I dare not contemplate.

Mick was an extremely heavy drinker and under the influence he could be extremely insulting, but he always got away with his boorishness. Even individuals known to use physical violence when aroused seemed to enjoy his barbs. Mick was very much the man's man and his persuasive charm quickly allayed anger. We often came near to blows. I'm not one for physical violence but one night at an engagement he incensed me so much I invited him to come outside and fight. I was so furious I was inclined to thump him on the spot but as I was the booker for this particular function, a college dance, precipitating fights with the bandleader I also represented would hardly be good for business. Leastways, that was my rationale for holding back. Mick affected his hurt-surprised look, demurred, but indicated that if I persisted in this hostility that he might well take me up on the invitation. It wasn't fear of me that restrained him. It was a late finishing dance and the bar was still open. This was a consideration to be put before and above all else.

He wasn't only a man's man. I've never known anyone who could attract and win the girls like Mick. With an urgent dedication somewhat lacking in his professional and business conduct he diligently applied an animal magnetism not to be gained from correspondence courses. Not that he was a smoothie of the hand-kissing variety, nor did flattery play much part in his astounding tally of successes.

" OH, I do love Mickie," gushed one young lady. " He's so delightfully grubby and you know exactly where you stand with him."

Indeed on both counts. An extremely handsome buck he was nevertheless extremely careless about his appearance. He rarely cleaned his teeth. " I'm the last of the Emerald Green Brigade," he informed a lady reporter from an evening newspaper, who quoted this admission.

Amorous gentlemen who would bathe regularly, clean their teeth and fingernails, anoint themselves with various deodorants and eschew bad language in the presence of the desired one, would gape in disbelief that a drunken, hard-swearing figure should so effortlessly charm the girls.

The direct approach was half his success. Attractive (and some not so attractive) girls would be left in no doubt about Mick's intentions. His invitation to fornicate—not that he employed such formal phraseology—was a successful shock tactic and Mick confirmed my long-held belief that women, all women, of all ages, are fascinated by rakes. Point one out to a woman at a party and watch her gravitate, perhaps unconsciously, as if by some primeval instinct, in his direction, and Mick's sexual reputation was indeed a magnet to the ladies.

The band played an engagement at the Royal Festival Hall for a famous charity organization. It was a ' class ' engagement that could have resulted in similar bookings had the band made a good impression. That afternoon I urged Mick not to get drunk. That entreaty was a mistake. He would probably have got drunk anyway but a request of this nature, particularly from me, would mean that he'd do precisely the contrary.

He arrived at the Festival Hall with eyes glazed and palpably swaying. Although he had paced his drinking throughout the afternoon and was well practised in concealing his intoxication he, like most soaks, couldn't accurately judge when it was too late to pretend sobriety. This evening the alcohol was well in control. We had a row. When I get angry, I mispronounce and in this heated exchange " lackadaisical " popped out as " lack-sadiacal " and Mick gleefully seized upon the error. I spluttered with rage and Mick imitated my stutter. Just then he came extremely close to being thumped without any formal invitation to step outside, despite the physical consequences to myself, and regardless of how a fracas would affect the engagement; but, within minutes, the boiling anger was replaced with utter incredulity.

Christopher Chataway, then known as a world-famous athlete, was present with an extremely attractive, well-cleavaged girl. Chataway was handsome, smart, undoubtedly well-scrubbed and looked the picture of an assured, successful man escorting a lovely girl. It wasn't long before the girl, who hadn't met Mick before, was running her hands through his matted locks. Mick's eyes gleamed through the beery glaze and the Emerald Greens flashed like those of the pantomime devil when he's just about to embrace the despairing heroine, except that the lady here looked anything but despairing. Quite the contrary. Chataway was not amused. Had he discovered that Mick's politics were his, I doubt if this would have been much of a consolation. There are chemical factors that transcend the strongest political affinities. I had the utmost difficulty in getting Mick to the bandstand. His thoughts were far removed from playing the trumpet. Once the session was under way the band was the success of the evening, the other bandleader of the evening, Ken Mackintosh, quite put out by the reception they received.

On an earlier occasion the band had a spot on one of the bandleader Ted Heath's ' Swing Sessions ', held every Sunday afternoon at the London Palladium. Mick arrived very drunk but sensibly employed the concealment technique of keeping silent. Had he spoken, it would have been confirmation of what the band and I already knew and what Heath eventually suspected. In his cups Mick's complexion and eyes were his giveaway. The former went a greasy-grey, the latter heavily glazed. Mick, not normally one to be easily impressed, was rather in awe of Heath and didn't attempt any of his usual insinuating ploys to pre-empt any criticism about his condition. The band played their three numbers without any mishap. Mick was in control—just. Afterwards Heath sternly told me that if Mick had been drinking he wasn't to take the customary bow with the rest of the bill. In refuting the suggestion that Mick was drunk I did my best to sound convincing and at the same time rather hurt at the very idea and Mick took the bow. Had he plunged into the orchestra pit below I wouldn't have been the least bit surprised. Certainly it would have made for a more enjoyable finale than all that show-biz beaming and bowing.

Heath, a teetotaller and highly successful dance band leader with sixteen musicians, and Mick, a boozer and struggling jazz band leader with only five, had at least one thing in common. Both had three vocalists.

Mick's penchant for supernumerary personnel was one of his more extraordinary indulgences. In his first band he had two banjos when every other band was content with one, the additional player hired " because he's a good nut, cock ".

Mick could have been a much better trumpeter than he was. He had an exceptionally strong lip and on his good days he played with considerable power and feeling, but he rarely

E

bothered to practise and had an almost pathological objection to rehearsals.

With the most honourable of intentions his clarinettist Archie Semple, George Melly and myself conspired to get Mick round to my office, where we stressed the necessity for rehearsals. Mick was furious. This was ' disloyalty ', a heinous crime in his book. Very much in the manner of a Victorian patriarch reprimanding a presumptuous servant, I was told to mind my own business.

It was an odd contradiction in Mick's character that such a hell-raiser bucking against social and musical conventions should be so autocratic in anger, so right-wing in his politics and so incredibly Victorian in his attitude to women, the latter characteristic contributing much to his success with that sex. He had a Victorian attitude to those who had fallen, even if he had personally contributed to their downfall.

He developed a technique, necessary for a man as remiss as himself, of keeping a mental ledger of other people's failings. Recorded in detail they would lie, gathering interest as it were, until the opportunity came for him to read them out, having no scruples about their irrelevancy in a particular argument, and if he probed a sore point he would jab at the wound without mercy. But the charm was beamed on if he felt magnanimous in victory. That charm! It worked wonders on dance hall managers, agents, promoters and public alike. It had to. His band was often unrehearsed, frequently late and sometimes drunk. Despite these shortcomings (or maybe because of them) the band had a steady following. Their ravers' charisma compounded of much drinking, casual sex, bad language and iconoclastic attitudes, appealed to fellow spirits and also, typically, to many whose life-style was sober and moral.

It wasn't easy doing business with Mick. He was a law unto himself. He deliberately delayed his decisions, was obdurate in his refusal to rehearse, wouldn't keep appointments I made with, or for, him and was forever tardy in returning his contracts.

" I've got them in an envelope (stamped, addressed, by me, to me) on the mantelpiece, all signed, cock," he would say and that's where they stayed, the actual posting of the envelope a mighty hurdle he rarely managed to overcome.

He was extremely slow in settling his commission accounts, a matter of great import to an agent. Not that he tried to evade settlement. Mick was a hundred per cent honest in money matters; he was just too bone idle to write out a cheque. Often I would retain a cheque made out for him and strike a balance but, inevitably, we disagreed about the arithmetic. Mick, as an excuse, always claimed I was late in submitting my accounts, any errors on which, he asserted, always happened, just by chance, to be in my favour. These disputed amounts could be as low as ten shillings, which in those days could buy five pints of bitter, the precise purchasing possibility of that sum in Mick's mind.

Under the influence he would phone and harangue me over trivial issues. The following morning, sober, he had completely forgotten his complaints. This was the tenor of our relationship for a decade. It was anything but straightforward but other experiences at the time made Mick seem, in comparison, a knight in shining armour.

In addition to the traditional jazz bands and a few ' modern ' small combinations some big dance bands were touring the country, two of these led by Ambrose and Roy Fox. Both had been household names in the 'thirties. Both had made and lost vast fortunes. Both were trying to scratch a living playing one-night stands. Both were instrumentalists. Ambrose played violin, Fox the trumpet, but neither were good enough musicians to play in another band, or play ' sessions ' in recording and broadcasting studios, even if their pride would have let them. They were having an unhappy time. The jazz bands were taking an increasing bite of the available business and most of the big bands, bowing to current fashion, were employing Be-bop stars, these often reluctantly making their bread and butter in such employment and allowed only the occasional solo.

Although traditional jazz borrowed heavily from the past it was, in a sense, as much a music of the time as Be-bop. Ambrose and Fox had dated associations, although the former had un-comfortably dabbled with modern style arrangements and Be-bop stylists.

Successful agent Harold Davison suggested co-representation of Ambrose and, unwisely, I jumped at the chance, even though ' co-representation ' meant a smaller share of the commission.

Davison introduced me to this colourful character in his Mayfair
flat. " Ammie " was a legend in his own time, and I was rather
in awe of him when the introduction was made. Mock Grecian
urns were spread around a somewhat garishly furnished lounge
and as he wearily flicked cigarette ash into the nearest urn he
candidly admitted that he had squandered a fortune estimated
by many at over a million pounds and this at pre-war values.
" It all came too easily," he said. " I had no understanding of its
value." Also present was his secretary. She had the hauteur of
a duchess. Perhaps she was a duchess. Ambrose had been a
friend of the aristocracy in his hey-day and maybe she was a
loyal duchess.

   " We've not heard of you before, Mr Godbolt," she said. It
was when she made this observation for the third time I felt
constrained to murmur that she, too, had not impinged upon my
consciousness until that moment. Ambrose told her to shut up
and I liked him for that.

   Bert Ambrose had style. Born in the East End of London he
played mediocre violin but rose to become an international name
employing only the best musicians, some of them recognized
jazzmen. Whilst rubbing shoulders with royalty and society at
exclusive night clubs, he was also an idol of the masses, his records
selling in thousands, his broadcasts occasions on which the nation
stayed in. Before the war he took his band to Deauville, Cannes
and Monte Carlo, played before the crowned heads of Europe,
later gambled with them at the casinos, losing it was reported,
£20,000 in one night. Now, in 1953, he was over fifty, broke
and balding and had to take a band on the road merely to pay
his way. I didn't feel sorry for him on that account, but I warmed
to him for a frank approach and an undeniable presence.

   I didn't warm to the duchess, who was put out that a big
agent like Davison was delegating the booking of her Ambrose
to someone like me, someone—and she said it again—she'd
not previously heard of. Nevertheless she wanted to know when
I would be coming up with the big money jobs, seemingly unaware that conditions had changed since he reigned supreme.
There were no more residencies in night clubs for him. Although
these plush establishments still existed, the budgets were too
tight in those days of comparative austerity for the luxury of a

baton-waving, old-style bandleader—every man had to be an instrumentalist. The kind of glitter and affluence he had known in the 'thirties had disappeared. Indeed, some of the sons and daughters of his old 'society' admirers were now hurling themselves around the dance floor at 100 Oxford Street to Humphrey Lyttelton's band for the admission price of a few shillings.

Ambrose loathed one-night stands as much as he loathed the wild men of Be-bop his fixer sometimes employed, many of them straight from the Club Eleven in Gt Windmill Street, the cradle of the bop movement in this country. He bemoaned their behaviour in the band coach. " Farting and belching contests," he murmured, sadly shaking his head. " *Savages*," he added with acerbic vehemence.

He had arrived at one ballroom in the north of England to discover that the ' advertising' of his appearance consisted of his name chalked on a blackboard in the hall foyer. No glittering neon shimmered his name, no respectful uniformed doorman to assist him out of a chauffeured limousine—only this chalk scrawl to greet him after a journey of 250 miles in a trippers' coach hired for the day.

It was the writing on the wall as well as the blackboard for Bert Ambrose. Instead of the West End and Riviera fleshpots, his round was now the King's Hall, Clitheroe, The Drill Hall, Workington, The Casino, Warrington and not blowing up a storm in any of these dismal halls. Instead of playing to aristocratic swells and their elegant ladies, his audiences were Teddy boys and girls, and the prospect of a farting match on the way home.

Ammie was frequently interviewed by the musical and national press. They were interested in a man who had been as rich as Croesus, but was now being pursued by creditors, including the landlord of that Mayfair flat. In one of the interviews he referred to the days when he tried to make a comeback, how things went badly for him, and that he had for an agent a " young man equal to the occasion ". I'm not certain he was referring to me, for he had many agents, but it could easily have been me. I didn't exactly steer him back to the golden highway.

This interview was printed in one of the more popular Sunday newspapers I don't normally read and I was obliged to George Melly for drawing the report to my attention. It might otherwise have escaped me.

Roy Fox, long cocooned in night clubs, waving his baton in front of silver and gold-plated trumpets and saxophones and a tier of violins, approached me after it became known I was representing Ambrose, but his band was equally difficult to sell. In fact I spent a lot of time and money trying to sell the unsaleable.

Because it was a fact I was representing these orchestras I was prevailed upon to represent a newly formed big band. When the leader came to my office he warmly shook my hand, fixed me with big blue eyes and avowed that I was his man. I subsequently discovered that the reason for him approaching a small-time agent like me was that all the bigger offices had turned him down.

He claimed an inexhaustible supply of capital from a backer to sustain the venture. This backer soon withdrew his support and without funds other than limited band earnings the band ran into financial trouble.

There was almost a different personnel each night, musicians leaving when they didn't get paid. This bandleader had an appealing earnestness and persuasive manner that was most impressive, but these smooth blandishments would soon change to harsh words, especially under the influence of drink. In one of our heated exchanges he threw out the hoary old saw about agents being " bloodsuckers ".

" It's people like me," he roared, "who keep bastards like you in a living," rather overlooking the large sum in commission he owed me, not to mention four pounds for a telephone call to Cairo. This charge was the end product of a publicity stunt his road manager had engineered, although the bandleader, a humourless and self-deceiving individual, probably convinced himself that the exercise was for real.

The manager had read that the recently deposed King of Egypt, Farouk, had a sister who was a night-club singer and he hit on the idea of offering her a job with the band. The very notion that an Egyptian princess, albeit one no longer enjoying

regal status, would leave her native land to sing in the Drill
Halls, Palais and Corn Exchanges with a bandleader she didn't
even know was bizarre enough, but it also revealed how gullible
the press and its readers were in regard to the band business.
About a dozen representatives of the Press packed into my
office one phantasmagoric afternoon and a telephone call was
put through to a Farid El Atrash in Cairo. Mr Atrash was the
link man in this charade and I recall the name so clearly, probably because I was charged four pounds for the call.

My supply of drink was soon consumed by thirsty pressmen
and, wanting a full audience for a drama-charged entry, the
bandleader arrived late. He wore an expensive-looking, tight-
fitting Crombie overcoat and a Homburg hat—formal wear
suitable for an occasion that was to be a landmark in the history
of British dance music.

As this stunt was going to result in a stupendous increase in
business the bandleader thought the cost of the call should be
my contribution to the exercise. I still have a copy of the bill.
In my recent poverty-stricken years when I could have made
good use of four pounds I often mused that this was the price of
my involvement, albeit tenuously, with the sister of a deposed
monarch.

When I told Mick about these misadventures his eyes gleamed.
"Oh, we're not such a bad lot after all, then!" a meaningful
observation bearing on my repeated criticisms of his behaviour.
Too true! For the next ten years I stuck to jazzmen as business
acquaintances and, with one exception, I didn't encounter the
sort of difficulties, trickery and chicanery, not to mention the
chutzpah I had unhappily experienced with the has-beens and
would-bes.

I acquired a few clients during this period. Clients are very
important to an agent. He can book his own bands into their
venues and claim a full ten per cent of the total fee. He can
book other agents' bands into these venues and claim five per
cent. No charge is made to the client for his booking services.
The agent is only too happy to oblige.

My first client was Duncan McKinnon, operating from
Melrose, a rumbustious man as resolutely brave as he was mul-

ishly stubborn. He was the first to book jazz bands in the Scottish borders and he obsessively spent vast sums trying to establish the Market Hall, Carlisle, as a viable dance hall proposition. He booked the biggest names in the country but this bleak and cavernous structure reeking with the odour of rotting vegetables defied his valiant endeavours. He would harangue bemused audiences about his intentions and recite vast excerpts from Robert Burns to support his pronouncements, but to no avail. A flamboyant and lovable character and as genuine a person as I've ever met, if over-fond of malt whisky, his support was a great help to me in those early, difficult days as a band agent.

7

CHEAP AND CHEERFUL

After parting from the Wilcoxes, Humphrey Lyttelton continued to play at 100 Oxford Street on Wednesday nights under the name of the Humphrey Lyttelton Club. By the end of 1952 his office was promoting at these premises seven nights a week.

Only soft drinks were available in the club room, a dowdy, oblong basement with faded reproduction murals of sylvan scenes on the walls—it was a restaurant by day—and alcoholic refreshment was sought at the 'Blue Posts', a pub at the corner of Newman and Mortimer Streets, about two hundred yards around the nearest corner.

The 'Posts' was the fraternity's meeting-place before entering the club, although once a heavy drinking session started there were many who frequently didn't manage to hear a note. Some, flush with William Younger's Scotch Ale, would scurry to make the last number or, hopefully, one of the club's beauties.

The 'Blue Posts'–100 Oxford Street nexus was a *scene* with a distinctive atmosphere. A new camaraderie had emerged. Many young record collectors had become instrumentalists, some on a full-time basis and playing as they pleased. The odd waltz and a very brief version of the National Anthem were the only concessions to Palais requirements.

A phrase used by those newly emergent professionals was, " It's better than working,"—even though they were travelling hundreds of miles a week. However, they remained essentially amateur in character. To play traditional jazz was still something of a crusade, although it had become accepted by the entertainment business generally. Agents and promoters, hitherto uninterested, were asking for jazz bands. " It's trad I want," said one agent to me, "something cheap and cheerful." The abbreviation 'trad' soon became the accepted label and much disliked by many revivalists for its associations with a stereotyped formula.

The instrumentation was invariably trumpet, trombone, clarinet, piano, bass, drums and banjo, the latter instrument a prominent insignia of the style. The routines were one or two choruses of the theme collectively improvized, a sequence of solos and more collective choruses for a rousing finish. The tunes were almost invariably those recorded by the New Orleans giants and, in some cases, the routines and solos directly copied from records.

The standards of musicianship had improved considerably but there are some quite hilarious records of bands who rushed into recording studios all too prematurely.

Despite a general uniformity of instrumentation and style there were differences in style, the merits of each school protested with some fervour.

'Dixieland' was also a term disliked by the revivalists. This suggested 'white' jazz (such as the Original Dixieland Jazz Band, the first jazz band to be recorded, all of whose musicians were from New Orleans but white), especially as pre-war dance-band musicians like Sid Phillips and Harry Gold had jumped on the bandwaggon and formed bands playing 'Dixieland', a term derisively used by Be-bop musicians (some of them able, if unwilling, members of conventional dance bands) to describe the music of the revivalists, who preferred the appellation 'New Orleans', this being suggestive of the coloured style (although all the revivalists were white). The revivalists in turn continued to employ the word Be-bop, knowing how much its practitioners hated it, preferring their music to be known as 'Modern Jazz'.

This is an attempted simplification of a terminological confusion that might have got the lexicographers in a tangle, had they been interested. It is perhaps significant that, with the odd exception, no British coloured people and very few Jewish persons were revivalists. Both coloured and Jewish were active in 'Be-bop'. (In the United States not *one* single young coloured instrumentalist embraced revivalism.)

Modernists were sharp dressers—sartorial identification with a music a lot more complex than Trad. Trad musicians rarely took drugs, apart from socially and legally acceptable alcohol and nicotine. Some Be-bop musicians took illegal drugs, with a few tragic consequences.

There was a school of thought and action well to the left of the average revivalist. It was comprised of critics, fans and musicians who had a zealous allegiance to the primitives of American jazz.

The primitives' unexpected rise to fame in their late years is one of the most romantic stories in jazz history. In the 1920s most of the New Orleans musicians migrated north and made their classic ' New Orleans ' recordings and international fame in Chicago and New York. Amongst those who stayed in New Orleans were trumpeter Bunk Johnson and clarinettist George Lewis. After an extraordinary series of events, resulting from a letter addressed to Bunk Johnson " c/o Post Office, New Iberia " from two American jazz critics in 1937, he was first recorded in 1942 at the age of sixty-three. George Lewis was then forty-two. Both were working in humble jobs during the day and Johnson was so impoverished he couldn't afford false teeth and, allegedly, had to refuse his first offer to record on this account.

Johnson's first records made a sensational impact. The music, technically crude and patently out of tune had a rough power, a pristine innocence and a naïve charm that was almost pre-jazz by accepted standards.

Johnson continued to play up until his death at the age of seventy and Lewis led bands up to his death when he was sixty-seven. This folk artist from a harsh and poverty-stricken background became a cult hero throughout Europe and parts of the East, Japan particularly. His was a moving success story and his style, with its distinctive sonorities and singing tone, was probably the most imitated of all jazz clarinettists in the revivalist era.

In the ' Blue Posts ', Newman Street, London W.1., a far cry from New Orleans, the sincerity and *purity* of the Johnson-Lewis bands was fiercely declaimed, especially after a few pints of Younger's Scotch Ale. They were favourably compared with their more successful New Orleans kinsfolk like Louis Armstrong and Sidney Bechet who had achieved fame earlier.

The poor were exalted, the successful—especially the white musicians—were derided. The hungry background of the primitives—particularly appealing to well-fed critics—imbued them with a rare saintliness. There were racial factors : Johnson's not being able to afford teeth was a symbol of white oppression.

The purists were obsessed with the concept of instrumental purity. They hated the saxophone. The three-part polyphony of ' true' jazz, performed by trumpet (tenor), clarinet (soprano) and trombone (bass), best exemplified by the Johnson-Lewis bands, was the holiest of jazz verities and if a saxophone squirmed, serpent-like, into this ensemble to sully its purity, it had to be cast out. There was an Old Testament fervour about these intense proclamations.

The Johnson-Lewis style, so seemingly antiquated, was devoutly emulated by many young white musicians halfway through the century.

The foremost disciple and exponent of this style in this country (and elsewhere, including the United States) was the London-born trumpeter, Ken Colyer. The " Guv'nor ", as Ken was affectionately called, was utterly, almost fanatically devoted to the jazz of his choice. His burning passion for his heroes was exemplified in a way quite untypical of a bandleader. An admirer approached him and unwisely expressed the opinion that his, Colyer's, band was better than George Lewis's. Ken looked incredulously at his flatterer and promptly thumped him for such unforgiveable heresy.

In the early 'fifties Ken signed as deck-hand aboard a merchant ship, but only with the motive of paying homage at the shrine, New Orleans. There he jumped ship, was eventually jailed and deported but not before he had played with George Lewis and others, defying the rigid colour bar that still exists in a city whose most famous sons are its coloured jazz musicians.

Ken suffering imprisonment to play with the Gods elevated him to the Pantheon. So revered, he made a triumphant return to lead a band specially formed in his absence. Chris Barber was on trombone.

Ken was in an earlier band led by the Christie brothers. They couldn't find a suitable drummer and, as a temporary measure, his brother Bill came in on washboard. Bill, as fanatical as his

brother, was given to impassioned sermonizing. We met one
night at 'The Posts' and he came at me with all ideological
guns blazing. " I know I'm not exactly what the Guv'nor wants,
mate, but until he finds a drummer who understands the sound
he's after I'll be there with my bleeding knuckles bleeding, mate."
He held up his chafed knuckles and glowered at me, a deviationist
who had expressed a liking for Lyttelton's band.

"Yes, mate, if I have to tear these knuckles to the bone I'll
be there and, mate, he needs all the help he can get with the
rest of the bastards screwing him up."

The "rest of the bastards" were the other members of the
band. This was hardly surprising as Keith Christie had developed
an interest in modern jazz and a year or so later was in Johnny
Dankworth's Big Band.

Ken, the fervent purist, also had differences over musical
policy with the band formed in his absence and soon departed.
Chris Barber became leader. With some changes of personnel
and modification of the purist policy the band became an international attraction earning a lot of money.

Had anyone forecast to me a year or so earlier that Chris
was going to be the leader of a highly successful band I would
have fallen about with maniacal laughter. When Chris broke
as a big name I may have allowed the odd rueful smile to pucker
my normally taut lips, but I didn't fall about laughing, not with
all that commission going to another agent.

Representatives of all styles appeared in a concert at the Royal
Festival Hall staged by the National Federation of Jazz Organizations in the presence of H.R.H. Princess Elizabeth. Those responsible for Her Highness's surprising patronage were an Irish
peer, the Marquis of Donegal, and the Honourable Gerald
Lascelles, a cousin of the Princess.

A jazz concert attended by the next in line for the Throne at
the invitation of two blue-bloods and an ex-Etonian band leader
on the bill caused a flurry in Fleet Street. The Press was jolted
by this seal of royal approval. Jazz became news. The fraternity
were treated with many priceless gems in those ' society ' columns
which impart to the poor the junketings of the rich.

In the *Evening Standard* we read of a coming-out ball in

Kensington where the guests included a Lady Jane Wallop, a Lady Chetwynd-Talbot, a Mr Richard Tatham and a Mr Jeremy Grafftey-Smith and these two latter " sent a row of flower pots bordering the band-stand over like skittles as they joined the band for a jive number ". This entertainment was followed by " Mr Grafftey-Smith giving an imitation of Louis Armstrong singing ". We were entranced by the report that the eighteen-year-old Duke of Kent " tried his hand at the drums " on one of these sprauncy occasions, and that Princess Alexandra did the same. Other guests followed suit and " soon there was a queue of volunteers to play ' Hot ' [the newspaper's quote marks] jazz numbers."

Hoorays " having a go on the drums " was quite common-place. These, and the string bass, were instruments apparently playable without any tuition. You never heard of the odd Honourable or Duke " trying his hand " at playing the saxo-phone.

There was a report that H.R.H. Princess Elizabeth, now regarded by the Press as a jazz fan, was attending a small dinner party in Cadogan Square and that one of the guests, actress Jane Carr, was going to entertain on the piano, the report solemnly adding that Miss Carr was equally adept at the classics and jazz.

Miss Carr's prowess at the latter, either on record or by word of mouth, hadn't reached the jazz fraternity then, or since, but perhaps there are some gems of private recordings waiting to be discovered and if they are their background ensures maximum publicity.

In the late 'forties, and throughout the 'fifties, Riverboat Shuffles were annual events. These emulated, in spirit at least, a former Mississippi institution, the giant riverboats that once steamed up and down that mighty river from New Orleans to places as far north as Davenport, 942 miles as the crow flies, many employing jazz bands.

The British successors to these Mississippi steamboats were Thames pleasure boats plying from Richmond, Surrey, to Chertsey, Surrey, some six miles, and back again, with British trad bands performing. If the sun shone and with the bars being open all day these events were great fun.

The papers usually sent a reporter and cameraman along. With the constant jiving aboard and on the river banks, with much billowing of skirts and some of the girls dancing in their bikinis, it was enough, in those days, to have the reporters agog with the 'lasciviousness' of it all.

One young lady reporter from the magazine *Illustrated* got quite carried away. Under the heading "Old Jiver Thames" she wrote, "The boat contained 250 of the London Jazz Club's wildest members . . . the bands tom-tommed all the way from Richmond to Chertsey . . . Bob Barclay's ragtime tuba almost drowned the ship's siren calling enthusiastic be-bop dancers from the river banks . . . they had left the ship to cut a couple of rugs . . . this is where the fans forget their Iron Curtain blues and dance. . . ." We used to enjoy the wild and immoral associations the press consistently engendered. When introduced as "jazz fiends", young ladies would back away, children hid behind mum's skirts. At least that's what we hopefully looked for. There was no point in being a "fiend" if there wasn't a frightened reaction.

We were conscious of our separateness, and very happy about it. It was a pleasure to be separated from the fans of Ted Heath, Edmundo Ros, Harry Secombe and Liberace.

Like other minorities we developed an argot of our own. It was a mixture of American jazz and cockney rhyming slang and some Australianese left behind by the expressive Mel Langdon. My introduction of 'Hooray Henry' was developed and Henry's female counterpart was a 'Henrietta', often abbreviated to 'Hetty'. Henry's working-class opposite was an 'Erbert', his lady an 'Emma'. 'Hooray' soon applied to cars, areas, certain sports, clothes, speech and, most of all, social and political attitudes. It was a handy class label. A 'cheer' of Hoorays and their Hettys were immediately identifiable on the dance floor at 100 Oxford Street. Their extraordinary antics were the comic spectacle of the jazz scene. Conversely, it was an odd sociological fact that the 'Erberts' and 'Emmas' were almost all rhythmic and disciplined in their movements. A sense of timing, a feel for rhythm was necessary for jive dancing. What looked uncontrolled was, like the music that inspired it, highly disciplined.

The Hoorays were congenitally incapable of realizing this. Humphrey Lyttelton in his book *Second Chorus* mentions one in particular. He would leave his partner and charge around the floor like a rogue elephant. Hetty would remain stationary but swaying, mouth agape and eyes fixed on the ceiling as if in a trance. Returning to her after his solo charge around the floor, Henry would grab her arm as if to remove it from its socket and they'd resume their elephantine cavortings.

In the ' Blue Posts ' during the interval their strident honks pierced the buzz of ordinary conversation. We got to know their real names.

" Arabella! What would you like to drink?" Arabella was bedraggled and perspiring, having been roughly hurled about by her escort. These Hoorays treated their women with quite ungentlemanly brutality.

" Oh, Gideon, I'm so FRIGHTFULLY thirsty. A H-UGE orangeade would be SOO-PAH!"

After a while the Hoorays and Hettys stopped coming to the club. They must have found another ' craze '.

The Hoorays and Hettys were the upper-crust representatives of the social spectrum. Sober-suited office-workers and professional men mingled happily with these and bearded, sandalled and duffel-coated students and factory workers. The girls were mostly office workers and art students, with the occasional heiress consorting with jazz musicians in the same manner that some of them thought it fun to associate with criminals.

' The Blue Posts ', a nondescript pub redeemed only by some superb Victorian engraved and gilded mirrors, had hitherto been a quiet place in the evenings, its clientele a sprinkling of porters and caretakers from nearby hotels and flats. When the jazz invasion hit them they gaped and wondered at the antics and the language of some of the more free-spoken of the fraternity.

One of the characters used to parade and caper in the distance between club and pub. Outside the pub doors he would play the trumpet to the intense annoyance of the landlady, a formidably shrewish woman. We used to know him as Martin Feldman and his antics were extremely unfunny.

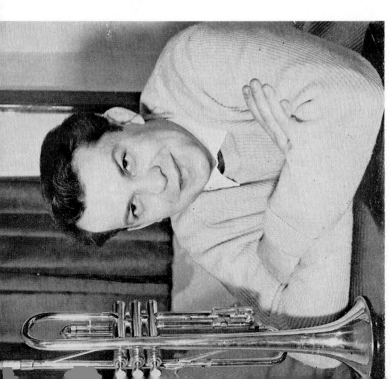

Mick Mulligan and Bert Ambrose
(Photos : source unknown and Melody Maker)

A study in jiving with
Pam Mulligan and
Monty Sunshine
*(Photo: Radio Times
Hulton)*

Chris Barber *(Photo :
Marquee Organisation)*

He has since risen to tremendous popularity, although not as a trumpeter. That Martin Feldman is Marty Feldman, one of the great comics of our time. None of us would have believed this possible in the 1950s.

Another character was drummer ' Herr ' Lennie Hastings. His speciality was to climb a table and do a splendid imitation of the fruity Austrian tenor, Richard Tauber. With his trousers legs rolled up and a monocle stuck in his eye he'd render " You Are My Heart's Delight " to rapturous applause.

Trumpeter Spike Mackintosh, after a scotch or two, would interlard his ecstatic praise of Louis Armstrong with vocal imitations of the great man's solos; Laurie Ridley, known as ' Jewish Laurie ', parodied his own intense Jewishness after a few ' sherberts '; Mulligan, outrageously, successfully, invited the birds to fornicate.

There were some I only knew by nickname. Les the Bohemium, Charlie the Pointer, Johnny the Conductor, Soppy Sid, Ray the Bopper, Bacon and Eggs, the Royal Oaf, the Pocket Romeo and the Singing Potato.

And the Ladies . . . Trixie, Susie, Katie, Pauline, Ro, Little Beryl and Big Beryl . . . Beryl Bryden, blues singer whom I first saw at the Public Jam Session in St John's Wood as far back as 1941 and still very active on the jazz scene.

There were girls who I knew only by their rather unflattering nicknames. Miss Uplift, the Horse, Ox-Eye Daisy (also known, allusively, as the Bicycle), Cow Pat, the Two Duckys, and two girls always together, one very large, the other diminutive, called the Whale and the Pilot Fish.

Behind the bar an old-style ' living-in ' spinster barmaid whose Red Indian cast of features earned her the sobriquet, The Squaw. She stood no nonsense from the Mulligan clique and silenced them with a freezing glance.

One of the many ex-public schoolboys on the scene was Jim Bray, sometime bassist with Lyttelton and Barber. Jim had been to St Paul's. We used to fence about class attitudes and conditioning. " Look at Godbolt," he would say, " he's managed to pull himself up by his boot strings."

Jim was notoriously scruffy, extremely well-read, and owned a large Rolls-Royce he had bought for £30. It once belonged

F

to King Zog of Albania, the royal arms displayed on the front doors.

I used to go for trips with Jim in this status-symbol vehicle and enjoyed the deferential attitude shown to the scruffy Bray by other drivers and policemen. As he had all the external appearances of a tramp they must have thought Jim an eccentric millionaire, surely convinced that no poor person would dare dress as badly as that. . . .

The average age of the clan moving from the club to pub and back again was mid-twenties but it wasn't unusual or thought out of place to see middle-aged men genuinely interested in the music and mixing with the younger people. You will not see any middle-aged people at rock and roll clubs.

There was glamour at the club. Joan Collins, then a starlet, looking utterly delectable in tartan trews and tight-fitting sweater, surrounded by eager young bloods, one of them clarinettist Cy Laurie who thought of himself as the reincarnation of New Orleanian clarinettist Johnny Dodds, and one of the few Jewish people ever to become prominent in trad jazz.

One night I danced with Diane Cilento. This was before she achieved fame as a film star. I asked for her telephone number. " Oh, you don't want my number," was the way she phrased her refusal. Her type, I discovered later, was more in the James Bond class when she married Sean Connery and, manifestly, I was not of the Bond calibre.

I remember all my dancing partners on that crowded steaming floor at 100 Oxford Street. The Dulcies, the Renes, the Junes, the Pats, the Muriels, the Bettys, the Sandys, the Joans . . . There were some truly lovely girls at the club, . . . or maybe distance lends enchantment to the memories of my youth. No matter, I'll stick with them. Now that I'm wretchedly middle-aged by God I'll stick to them!

Parties were always being hatched at the ' Blue Posts '. Addresses would be given, whispered or demanded. I gatecrashed one in a South Kensington mansion and danced with a coloured girl whose movements were a joy. She refused a second invitation maybe because I reeked of Scotch Ale or because of something I said. Whatever, the refusal was emphatic. This marvellous dancer I discovered years later was Shirley Bassey.

Much later I visited a flat in Portman Street that spawned a
national scandal. The occasion was a wedding reception for
one of my clients and given in this one-time residence of the late
Stephen Ward, one of the central figures in the Profumo case.
I noticed that the parquet flooring in the lounge was pitted from
end to end with the indentations of stiletto heels, indicating that
a large number of young ladies had been present at those purple
parties that led to a Cabinet Minister's downfall.

The three most successful bands spawned in the trad boom
were the three B's—Chris Barber, Kenny Ball and Acker Bilk—
and all three are still going strong.

The trad balloon swelled up to a considerable size and at one
stage there were some forty bands on the road, most of them
fully professional. Clubs sprang up throughout the country, with
all sorts of 'Erberts' running them, many of them given to
ideological pronouncements on 'true' jazz whereas, in truth,
their interests were strictly financial and to whom the sound of
the banjo was sweet music.

I tried to make a quick buck or two representing bands with
the banjo, but with little success. I employed the most devious
means to ease one of them into a major recording studio and
record a 'traddy-pop' single, but the record was never released.
Had it been and had it clicked, I doubt if the band would have
embraced or sustained any success, certainly not with the leader
it had.

One of the bandleaders, an assistant chef by trade, approached
me about 'going professional' and enquired, quite seriously,
if I thought he would be better off if he stayed in his job chop-
ping parsley. Yes, he would have been and it would have saved
me a lot of aggravation.

Lyn Dutton, my one-time partner, was the most successful
of the trad agents. His clients included Acker Bilk, Humphrey
Lyttelton, Chris Barber, Alex Welsh, Monty Sunshine, and many
more. Understandably, bands queued up to be represented by
such a successful agent. He was nicknamed " The Emperor ".

I owe a lot to Lyn and always found him to be a very fair
and reasonable person, even if we did have a few differences

and at one stage he was royally inaccessible. If I did manage to reach him by telephone or physically penetrate the fiercely protective cordon of receptionists and secretaries, enquiries for Acker engagements would have him yawning in boredom, a most enviable euphoria.

The trad phenomenon was truly quite extraordinary; the music of another era and a distant environment exhaustively researched, analysed, emulated, and, to a considerable degree, assimilated. It was the first ever example of a musical culture to be absorbed from gramophone records, and it was very exciting to be involved in the happening.

In the late 'fifties there was a reaction against trad. It fell into critical disrepute. The banjo, initially favoured by the revivalists for its ' cutting edge ' over the ' effete ' guitar dominated the entire rhythm section inducing staccato phrasing throughout. It was, without doubt, a very popular instrument. " Show me a banjo and you show me a profit " was the cry of one promoter and he spoke from the bottom of his heart.

The banjo's relentless chig-chug was only one unlovely feature of the stereotype that was being prettified in the recording studios to make ' traddy-pop ' records aimed for the ' Hit Parade ' and brutalized by rip-roaring tempos in the clubs for maximum excitement and applause.

From the rejection of the worst of trad came the style known as Mainstream.

8

CAREFREE MULLIGAN
AND TRUE-BLUE MELLY

"MULLY-MELLIGAN-TERRIFIC DIXIELAND MUSIC AND SUPERB DANCE ENTERTAINMENT" with the sub-heading "CAREFREE MULLIGAN and TRUE-BLUE MELLY" was the wording on a poster that faced Mick Mulligan and his band in the foyer of a Scottish dance hall on their arrival.

There was also a leaflet covering the entire tour with photographs of the alleged Carefree and True-Blue. It read: "Mick Mulligan, Debonair, Handsome and Hail-Fellow-Well-Met and George Melly, Artistic and Emotional singer of the Blues. Mick and George occupy and retain a place of their very own in the fantastic, unorthodox and altogether fascinating world of jazz".

It was, partly unintentionally, the most accurate of blurbs with "unorthodox" the operative word. They didn't come any more unorthodox than Peter Sidney Mulligan, educated Merchant Taylors, ex-Lt Oxford and Bucks Light Infantry and one-time director of a long established City firm of wine merchants and now jazz-band leader, and George Melly, educated Stowe, ex-Royal Navy Ordinary Seaman, art salesman and authority on Surrealism, now blues singer.

They were the terrible twins of jazz, both highly amusing and the perfect foil for each other, although not always in accord. In disagreement theirs was verbal jousting of a high order that had me, for one, helpless with laughter. Regrettably I find it impossible to convey any of these exchanges in print even if censorship and ordinary propriety would allow.

Mick, soft-spoken (officers don't shout), generally self-effacing and mostly friendly to everyone, although capable of caustic thrusts and unwarranted abuse. He was utterly without remorse.

George, loudly spoken, extrovert, generally friendly to everyone, but often patronizing and, in attack or defence, skilfully employed lifemanship at which the middle-class are so adept.

Both were from ordinarily respectable middle-class homes, both were completely amoral in their sexual behaviour. Mick was extremely right-wing in his politics and invariably unreliable; George was the apolitical anarchist and thoroughly dependable. Like two lovable knockabout comedians, Care-Free and True-Blue were on the road for twelve years, a unique liaison between two uniquely memorable characters.

The upsets between Mick and myself persisted. He had become George's personal manager and fancied himself more in this line than as a bandleader. He disbanded and entered into an agreement to become 'business manager' with another agent, but having contracts to fulfil he 'fronted' another band—led by Alex Welsh. Alex conveniently played trumpet and Mick, relieved for the most part of this tiresome chore, was able to leave the stand and engage in what he called 'soash-biz' (phonetic spelling, as near as I can get) meaning being sociable in the pursuit of business and usually involving a sharp movement towards the bar with the hall manager or owner.

It was a situation that produced many complications. One week Mick would appear at a venue with Alex's band and maybe in a week or so the same band, without Mick but sometimes with George, would appear at the same venue under Alex's name. When Alex wasn't available, a pick-up band under Mick's name appeared.

Whilst Mick was 'business manager' for another agency (I never discovered if he actually conducted any business) I was nominally Mick's agent, a confusing situation that tried my patience.

This arrangement soon folded and Mick was back on the road with his own band with George as vocalist and me as the agent, but Mick could still allow himself a word about the larger aspects of the business side.

His role, he told me in the Star Tavern in Charing Cross Road one night, was to fashion the grand design, and my job, as a functionary, was to implement the details. I asked him to elaborate. I was curious as to how the term " grand design " applied to booking a jazz band in palais and corn exchanges. At that moment someone he knew walked in and Mick greeted him with his usual mock-cockney, " Watcha gonna 'ave, then?" It soon developed into a heavy drinking session and Mick became too incoherent to impart details of his grand design and never got around to it, despite my further queries. I suspect it was no more than a transient whisp of a notion born of too many light ales.

Drink, the stimulant, the lubricant, the buttress, the catalyst. It was an integral part of Mick's activities.

It was inconceivable that we entered a tea-shop when the pubs were open. Had this ever been suggested to Mick, assuredly his jaw would have dropped in sheer disbelief.

Mick and George were interviewed for the *Melody Maker* by the late Maurice Burman, drummer and critic, at his flat. Burman quipped, " I hear you're a drinking duo."

" Not for the past fifteen minutes," was Mick's snappy rejoinder and Burman apologetically produced a bottle of gin kept for Christmas and special occasions. The guests soon polished off the contents.

The Mulligan Band were *the* top drinking band. No other band of topers could lay claim to this dubious title. Despite the effect alcohol had on their playing, despite it often fragmenting the handsome, debonair, hail-fellow-well-met demeanour of the leader, their renowned intake was undoubtedly part of their appeal.

When Mick and George were about things happened. Outrageous they may have been, but never dull, and these ravers had around them a band noted for their idiosyncracies. Indeed, they were a rare assortment.

In George Melly's book *Owning Up*, it appears that Mick thought I had my share of idiosyncracies, not that I had to read this very funny chronicle of a jazz band on the road to be aware of Mick's sentiments.

George asked my permission to use the stories about myself.

I can't say I was overwhelmed with pleasure when I read the original draft but there were one or two fairly complimentary references which slightly mollified me. However, Diana Melly, who was editing the book, cut out these references before my very eyes, leaving me like the film actor agonizingly watching his best scenes fall in celluloid curls to the cutting-room floor.

Since publication I've had all manner of people from far and wide, some totally unconnected with the business, eagerly, gleefully saying, " I've been reading about you " as if I had been on trial for some awful offence and, referring to one story, asking, " Had any good nightmares lately?" I have even been invited to parties on the strength of my oddities being mentioned in *Owning Up*, a claim to fame I could well do without.

I first saw George at the London Jazz Club cavorting about the dance floor in the wild Hooray fashion and, without giving myself any credit for being particularly observant, I knew we had a posturing exhibitionist in our midst. In ' The Blue Posts ' during the band's interval I could hear his declamatory bellowing above the hum of normal conversation. It was plain that we were to be his audience, like it or not.

I also observed a considerable vanity hardly in keeping with an appearance that was never Byronic, a self-esteem that showed no signs of abating as the girth and jowls increased. " He thinks he's the last red bus home," tartly observed a barmaid at a drinking club after George had tried to chat her up, but I soon discovered a very likeable, kind and highly intelligent man behind this flamboyant exterior and we became good friends. I was vastly entertained by his fertile imagery and brutally accurate mimicry and invited him to write for *Jazz Illustrated*. One contribution of his was a brilliant parody of " Jabberwocky " from *Through The Looking Glass*. Entitled " Jazzawocky " it summed up the difference in attitudes and dress between the traditionalist and the modernist.

I may not have foreseen Chris Barber as a successful band-leader, but I did recognize George Melly's potential as a writer.

The title of George's book is the jazzman's term for self-honesty and very much a part of his ethos, but it took a long time for George to own up. There was a time when he would have accepted that barmaid's tart observation that he was indeed the " Last Red Bus Home " although I fancy he would have preferred a more exotic simile.

For thirteen years George wrote the script for Wally Fawkes' strip cartoon, ' Flook ', in the *Daily Mail* and there were occasions, maybe unconsciously, when he tended to perhaps overlook Wally's contribution.

Wally was in a Chelsea pub when he was asked what he did for a living. Wally's reply naturally mentioned Flook. The questioner's eyes narrowed. He looked hard and long at Wally and said, menacingly, " Now look here chum, whoever you are, I'd be more careful if I were you. I happen to be rather a close friend of George Melly's."

Mick and the band quickly spotted this quirk of George's and would pointedly ask how *his* illustrator was behaving, enquire if the fellow was toeing the line, etc., etc., and affect not to remember his name.

And he could be most patronizing. We met in the King's Road, Chelsea, one Saturday, the day the ' Beautiful People ' make a ritual of parading this fashionable highway, heads constantly jerking from side to side to see and be seen. George was with a little clique of preening Chelseaites. He wore a wide-brimmed hat, a black cape and carried a silver-topped walking stick. He stared at me. " What on earth are *you* doing here?" he exclaimed as though I hadn't the right sort of credentials to use what, after all, was a public pavement.

Indeed he loved being amongst these ' Beautiful People '. He frequently joined them for what I mockingly described as " George's Little Dinners "—really quite prolonged and expensive affairs in chic Soho and Kensington restaurants with obsequious waiters encircling candle-lit tables and the rest of the flim-flams of ' good eating ', a striking contrast to the roadside greasehouses he was forced to patronize on tour.

Although passionate about the blues and sung with the utmost sincerity, I don't think George managed to assimilate the blues feeling. Other British singers, notably Sandy Brown and Long John Baldry, have been infinitely more successful in projecting a blues sound. It was as a showman that George excelled. His act, exhibitionistic and flamboyant, included exaggerated hand and body movements with much facial distortion and rolling of the eyes. In essaying the female role he stuck beer mugs up his sweater to simulate breasts and sang in a squeaky falsetto.

In his *tour de force*, " Frankie and Johnny ", he fell about and off the stage with quite alarming realism to lend emphasis to the line when Frankie shot her faithless lover down. It was a unique act; there was nothing like it anywhere. The voice and the movements were the camp Melly imbued with *bravura*, the theatricalism of the congenital show-off, but his announcements revealed a razor-sharp wit, his conversation and writing showing considerable erudition.

This was an intriguing combination of ham and intellectual. Understandably, he revelled in the surprise at the apparent contradiction.

I am writing of George as a performer in the past tense but in fact he is now (1975) enjoying greater popularity than ever before. In addition to singing to large audiences, he is writing book criticisms for *The Observer*, art criticism for *The Guardian* and appears regularly on the radio and television as a pundit. Such multifarious activities have attracted much attention and the novelty value of the contradictions persists.

In this permissive society which, by assiduous personal example, he has helped to foster, he's become a cult figure. He has been described in the *Melody Maker* by a young writer (no old jazz buff) as a " Super-Star of the 70s ", an unexpected accolade for a then forty-six-year-old raver after twenty-five years in the business.

George has long professed a hedonist's philosophy. In the austerity of the late 'forties and early 'fifties, coming after the relative puritanism of the 'thirties, George's bi-sexual promiscuity, heavy drinking and bad language were seemingly quite outrageous and much of it deliberately intended to shock. He can look back on himself as a pioneer of permissive behaviour, or ' raving ' as it was called in the jazz world. It was an infectious philosophy. A lot of people happily embraced it, although few were able to extend themselves with the panache of a Melly.

During the 'fifties I got my girlfriend, a potter, to strike special ravers' badges, to be awarded to top ravers. I was in my early 'thirties at the time and I go hot and cold at this recollection of an unduly protracted adolescence—somewhere about are ravers' badges as unfortunate proof of this. I assigned these badges and not seeing much of George at the time he wasn't awarded one. He was quite put out, but I explained I hadn't seen him as he was moving in more select social circles.

" True," he said with a chuckle. " My parties are now more Sloane Square than Stoke Newington."

Whilst I have derived much pleasure from watching George's act over the years, I still feel a twinge of embarrassment at the spectacle of an English, white, affluent, middle-class man singing the songs of the oppressed and poverty-stricken negro. I admit it's an illogical objection. I have no complaint about English, white, affluent middle (or upper) class men playing the blues through factory-manufactured instruments.

I didn't travel much with the band that now included my old room-mate the witty, waspish Ian Christie. I pleaded that I couldn't be up half the night and be at the office fresh and early to battle on their behalf. In truth I hadn't the moral fibre to face them too often.

It wasn't a camaraderie known for their exchange of sweet pleasantries. As a change from savaging each other, who better than their agent? They used to go for me like wolves round a sheep pen. One of the agent/band myths is the trip from Land's End to John O'Groats, or a similarly lengthy distance, in one day, arranged, it was alleged, by blindly stabbing pins into the map and fixing the engagements accordingly—or deliberately contriving this mammoth journey.

Against Mick I could sometimes retaliate with effect. Against seven of them, I stood no chance. I was a trafficker in human souls. Ensconced in my warm, cosy office these troubadours, travelling hundreds of miles a week cramped in a badly ventilated tin-box, were my victims. That's how they assiduously propagated the myth of the relationship.

On the occasions I entered the bandwaggon I saw, apart from the happy troubadours, every kind of detritus. It was never cleaned out and Melly's fussy and querulous attempts to keep it tidy were deliberately sabotaged by those determined that it should remain a mobile dustbin.

After one trip I left some large envelopes in the waggon. They were addressed to promoters and contained photos and write-ups of the band. It was obvious by the names and addresses what the envelopes contained and it might have been expected that one of the band, Mick particularly, would have picked them up and posted them. A week later I myself retrieved the envelopes, the addresses muddied beyond recognition. They had been stepped on innumerable times during that week.

But I had one or two memorable moments on tour. In one of Mick's first bands there was an Irish-Scots bass player called Pat Malloy. Pat, constantly beset with problems, frequently approached Mick with the dreaded words, " Perhaps we can have a little chat " and Mick would sit and suffer whilst Pat lengthily explained his problems, for even Mick wouldn't rubbish the kind and inoffensive Pat.

On one trip I was cornered by Pat. He presented me with a classically Irish poser. He had tax problems and for the purposes of his calculations would I, as I had access to diaries, let him have the date of every Friday for the previous five years. . . .

I accompanied the band to a party given by Lord Montagu at his ancestral pile at Beaulieu. I admit I liked the idea of seeing the inside of a stately home without having to queue up on Sundays with the rest of the proles. On the journey to Bournemouth where the band played a concert before the party, I sat next to Pete Appleby, the band's drummer and driver.

" You were in the Navy, weren't you, Bolt? So was I. What were you then? Oh! Ordinary seaman, eh?! I was an 'onorary officer. Mind you, the loot wasn't much. Only about twelves, but I 'ad me own batman." This intelligence was imparted with characteristic shaking of the shoulders. I recalled that honorary officers and batmen didn't figure in naval administration but remained silent. I wanted more of Pete's make-believe and enquired what his duties were as a honorary officer. He had the answer. " Ow! Just deciphering Russian code messages, things like that. Piece of cake, really." I was stunned by the fertility of his imagination. On this occasion he made no mention of his close friendship with " Phil ", otherwise Lt Philip Mountbatten,

R.N. later Prince Consort, with whom, Pete claimed, he was " like that " during his naval career. I liked Pete very much and admired the way he, a teetotaller, adjusted to the alcohol-induced changes of personality around him.

It was a dull party at Beaulieu, enlivened by Ian Christie rightly taking umbrage at the band being offered only that sickly beverage, brown ale, known for its proletarian associations and, presumably, ordered especially for the occasion. However, the band, and their agent, helped themselves to the more exotic drinks, and at Mick's urging—in contrast to his spirited defence of Montagu in the bandwaggon on the journey back to London.

Kenneth Tynan, one of the guests, had squeezed in for a lift and we got talking about cornettist Bix Beiderbecke. We both knew a superb solo of his on a record, " Sweet Sue ", by Paul Whiteman's Band and, as a change from the furious argument about the noble Lord's gaffe, we sang—or rather, in jazzman's fashion, burped—Bix's solo, only to be howled down by Christie, himself no admirer of Beiderbecke and still highly incensed at his Lordship's cheek in even thinking we would only expect brown ale. He sharply returned to the slight. George defended Montagu and the class war waged heavily in this cramped bandwaggon. Tynan was quite taken aback by the ferocity of the struggle.

" Why didn't you help yourself to the other drinks like the rest of us?" enquired George Melly.

" I can tell you why, George," Ian rasped sarcastically. " It's because I'm too humble."

" Don't be humble, dear boy," said Tynan. " You must stick up for your class."

In 1956 the band played a charity show in Wormwood Scrubs prison. Apart from a few nights in naval cells after drunken episodes, this was my first experience of being inside a jail proper. I vividly recall the all-pervasive sickly-sweet odour of sweat on rough serge worn by individuals in cramped and badly ventilated conditions. I remember being awed by the bleakness of the prison approaches and the immediate corridors once through the massive gates and realizing, above all, what occupation here entailed. That visit was in itself a deterrent for me to ever consider a crime punishable by imprisonment.

Before the band played, I chatted to a 'trusty' who was serving a life sentence for murder and it was his considered opinion, expressed with some glee, that another currently on trial for the same offence was due for a fate he indicated by going through the motions of a rope being tightly drawn around his neck. He made a deft grab at the fag-ends the band stubbed out as they mounted the improvized stage. This 'trusty' was also a 'baccy baron'. The band was a sensational success. Mick with impish delight, had chosen a programme appropriate to the engagement. " I'm Beginning to See The Light ", " Who's Sorry Now ", " After You've Gone " and " Keeping Out of Mischief Now ", were a few of the titles and George, camping madly, sprang on to the stage wearing an old-style convict's striped shirt to sing " Send Me To The Electric Chair " and other numbers with titles bearing on the current predicament of the audience.

The inmates roared their delight, especially at George's garb, excepting one youth with the coarse-grained features of a psychopath who sat utterly expressionless throughout, but I'm sure even he would have been won over had Mick chatted him. Mick could charm blood out of a stone, or humour out of a psychopath.

Three members of the Mulligan Band—Mick, trombonist Frank Parr, a brilliant wicket-keeper, former Lancashire C.C.C. professional, and once tipped for an England cap, and Pete Appleby—joined a jazzmans' cricket eleven called, appropriately enough, The Ravers. Although I had hardly held a bat in my life I turned out for a giggle one afternoon and, at the age of thirty-three, became hooked. In the twenty years since I've hardly missed a game.

Other members of the Ravers C.C. were Wally Fawkes, George Webb, Max Jones, Lyn Dutton, Jim Bray and Bruce Turner. It wasn't a joke side. Our cricket was played seriously, although not solemnly. In fact we soon gave up fixtures with show-biz elevens. The comics, singers and disc-jockeys in these sides thought the contests an opportunity to parade their chat, most of its abysmally unfunny and highly irritating on a cricket field.

Mick, myopic and frequently hung-over, was a superb close fielder, as quick with his catching and picking-up as he was with his wit. Pete, a good bowler, had an inordinately lengthy run-up quite superfluous for his medium pace, and when he took a catch he would dramatically roll over half a dozen times to ornament his feat. He lived his dream-world even on the cricket field.

Only Ray Smith, manager of a jazz record shop, Frank Parr, collectors Robin Rathborne and Andy Wheeler, trombonist Campbell Burnap and myself are the jazz remnants of a side that now includes city gents, a painter and decorator, two police inspectors, a Covent Garden vegetable salesman, a film lecturer, and others whose jobs and interests are far removed from jazz.

Melly and Christie were contemptuous of our involvement in this healthy exercise. Both were occupied with more cerebral matters that culminated in the former becoming film critic for *The Observer* and the latter for the *Daily Express*.

Ian was first with Les Perrin's office, then joined the *Daily Telegraph* and subsequently, the *Express*. Like photography and playing the clarinet, writing was something he seemed to take up with enviable ease.

He was always pressing for rehearsals and Mick hadn't lost his strong aversion to them. He eventually bowed to Ian's shrike-like (his nickname was Bird) pecking away at the issue and called a surprised band for rehearsal at the Metro Club in New Compton Street, off Charing Cross Road.

The persistent campaigner for more rehearsals arrived late and, rather drunk, wasn't in good shape to remember routines, both derelictions inwardly noted by an intensely watchful, testily sober Mulligan.

Halfway through a scratchy rehearsal author John Braine arrived at Ian's invitation and in a broad Yorkshire accent yelled, " Play ' Georgia ' in memory of dear old Nat," (Nat Gonella, British jazz trumpeter, famous in the 'thirties, whose signature tune was " Georgia ").

Nat was (and still is) very much alive, but Braine obviously thought he'd passed on. Mick eventually incensed by Braine's repeated cries for " Georgia " jumped off the bandstand, strode up to Braine and said, " Look here, cock, we don't tell you how to write fucking *Ulysses*, stop telling us what to play!"

In putting this unwanted audience of one at an unwanted rehearsal in his place, Mick also implied the superiority of James Joyce over John Braine. When Mick plunged the knife in he never failed to give it a wristy twist.

" Play ' Georgia '," gurgled Braine.

Mick said nothing to Ian at the time. The incident was an entry in the feared Mulligan ledger, to come in handy at a later date; which, of course, it did.

Some time after the abortive rehearsal Ian, hopeful that the incident had been forgotten, a vain hope considering the band-leader in question, again pressed for rehearsal.

" Oh, I'd like to, cock," blandly replied Mick. " But the chances are you'll get drunk (Mick was most censorious about drunkenness in others) and maybe invite some literary giant yelling for tunes we don't play. . . . Sorry, cock, I'd like to have a rehearsal, but it's the rest of the fellows, y'know, wasting their time. . . ."

On the night of the rehearsal I was at the ' Six Bells ', in King's Road, Chelsea, where I ran a jazz club in the upstairs room. I was standing at the top of the stairs hopefully peering down for the sight of paying customers when Ian and a man with a vaguely familiar face came unsteadily up the stairs.

No paying customers here, but I was rewarded in kind when Ian proudly introduced John Braine, paused, and perhaps feel-ing that I hadn't reacted as I should to the introduction, added, *Room At The Top*.

The Mulligan band had an ardent fan in a toper with the nickname of Fallabout Fred. Fred was attracted to the band's famed heavy drinking and fell, sometimes literally, into their company when they were in town. A none too tidy person, he had a particular fondness for gin, successive glasses of which were sunk in one gulp and with frantic rapidity if he were bent on reducing himself to a shambling absurdity, which was often.

There are hundreds of stories about Fred under the influence

George Melly
(Photo: T. A. Cryer)

Ravers Cricket Club, 1957, the first and only cricket XI comprised of jazz personalities. *Top row, left to right:* Pete Appleby, Bob Dawbarn, Jim Bray, the author, Mick Mulligan, Bruce Turner; *bottom row:* Frank Parr, Robin Rathborne, Wally Fawkes, Ray Smith

Don. *(Photo: Marquee organisation)*

John Cox ('Fat John')
and John Pritchard
(Photo : Crispin Enrich)

but I recall him, quite sober but bleary-eyed after the previous night's excesses, in a Soho pub waiting to take a young lady to the theatre. Fred didn't normally go in for 'fancy' pastimes like theatre-going but the show, *Black Nativity*, was one most jazz people went to see. His drinking that evening had been moderate, moderate for him, that is, and the girl arrived pert and pretty. She leaned forward.

"Do you like my perfume?" she asked. Fred sniffed suspiciously at anything as 'fancy' and fragrant as perfume. "It's O.K. I suppose," was his unenthusiastic reply.

"It should be, it cost me £2."

"How much!" cried Fred. "Two bloody pounds! What for, a pint?"

"No, silly, a phial. Perfume's expensive, you know."

"You've been bloody done," replied the gallant escort.

With an approach as unsubtle as this it was no surprise he was, at one time, having scant success with the ladies. When escorting them he frequently lived up to his sobriquet, leaving the girls with the impression he was more preoccupied with gin than themselves.

Unhappy about his lean patch, Fred, given to tears and confessionals in his cups, was lamenting his failures to one of the band's girlfriends.

"It's your own fault, Fred," she sternly replied. "You look so untidy and get so drunk. You're a good-looking chap and if you smartened yourself up a bit and cut down on the booze you'd do O.K."

At this sort of compliment Fred not only brightened up but felt encouraged. "All right then, how about a fuck?"

"Certainly not," replied the outraged young lady, and Fred exclaimed, "There! See what I mean!" And, bursting into tears, he fell down.

The Mulligan band's return to town was the unfailing signal for Fred's appearance. Even the band, themselves ardent topers, were embarrassed by his antics and confessionals.

When a film about the Mulligan band was researched, I met script-writer James Kennaway. He was at first horrified by the band's behaviour and they didn't take to his brash exterior which was difficult to equate with the author of such sensitive and

G

psychological novels as *Household Ghosts* and *Tunes of Glory*, the latter made into a memorable film, but they became reconciled and I got on well with him.

By sheer chance I met him in Majorca on one of my rare holidays and stayed with him and his wife Susan at a villa he had rented in a quiet part of the island. We got chatting about films and I related an incident at the Studio Club, in Swallow Street, near Piccadilly, a club at which quite a few members of the jazz fraternity gathered. Another member was Alexander McKendrick, film director, and one night I engaged him in conversation about films. I fancied I knew a lot about films. McKendrick, who had then spent twenty years in films and had achieved considerable fame as director of *Whiskey Galore*, *Mandy* and later *Sweet Smell of Success*, also knew a bit. I said my piece at wearisome length.

Later I was on the dance floor with Joan Biggs, my potter girlfriend, and shuffled in the direction of McKendrick. He was one of the most soft-spoken men I've ever known, but in a vibrant stage whisper that cleaved right through me he murmured to his partner, "Look out, here comes the film fan." Just then I would have had no difficulty in crawling into one of the hairline cracks in the tightly-knit parquet flooring.

"That's a coincidence," said Kennaway. "He's arriving here this evening. We're working on a script together." I went for a long walk. In my absence McKendrick arrived, was apprised of my presence, James describing me by the appellation McKendrick had given me.

McKendrick, as cool and detached as befits the public-school conditioning, just said, "Oh?" He was too polite, or overcome, to say more.

That evening I was practically mute when they were discussing films. For once I thought I had learned my lesson. Kennaway, a Scot, later invited me to a New Year's Eve party. It lasted the night and in the morning I was bleary-eyed, hung-over and undergoing the pangs of alcoholic remorse. Joan and myself were given coffee by a friend of the Kennaway family. "I hear that you are jazz people," she said, quite amiably, "and you seem to be quite intelligent."

On the surface this was an inane and patronizing remark but

it was no more than an expression of surprise, albeit that the compliment was doubly qualified and, painfully recalling my behaviour the night before, I couldn't be sure I would agree with her about myself, especially as I had forgotten my lesson at the Studio Club and had gone for the ear of another guest, Alexander McKendrick, about films. But jazz was a dog with a bad name and the stigma of association then still existed. Hence the lady's remark.

At one stage the band was receiving a fair amount of publicity. *The Sunday Times* carried an article entitled " A MAN CALLED MULLIGAN " and the *Melody Maker* a feature entitled " KING OF THE RAVERS ", both articles hinting at truths that couldn't be printed at the time (or now, even) but they were honest portraits of this Rabelaisian bandleader.

In *The Sunday Times* article I was described as a " gaunt, bowed hair-spring with haunted eyes ". How true : I had been Mick's agent for six years.

Mick was largely unaffected by the publicity. If he had been as commercially successful as Chris Barber, Acker Bilk and Kenny Ball I'm sure fame wouldn't have changed him much and, as far as I was concerned, he couldn't have been more difficult than he already was.

He was a genuinely unaffected person—not one for George's star-laced gatherings in N.W.1 or the swank restaurants. Gluttony was not a part of his animalism. A pie stall was more in his gastronomic line. It was one of the sights of Soho to see an intoxicated Mulligan accompanied by his bull terrier, Twist, both dining on meat pies at the coffee stall on the corner of Tottenham Court Road.

Mick's real vanity was his success with women. In sheer numbers he had an astonishing record. He didn't openly boast of his conquests (although he usually displayed them, some attractive, some a mere notch in the cock), but he did once say to me, apropos a certain young lady, " Even I haven't had that one ". It was an unguarded moment when he betrayed his pride in sexual conquest. His string of successes commanded the admiration of carnal man. There was a player in the band, a Northerner, who cried out to Mick one night in the bandwaggon,

" Yo full o' bloddy animule mugnetism!". It was a cry of envy more than a statement of fact.

He was quick to pounce if I erred or said a word out of place. Inspired by Louis Armstrong's moving version of the waltz, " I'll Never Walk Alone " I gauchely suggested that the band record a set of waltzes in jazz fashion. Of course, this was something that only an artiste of Armstrong's talents could attempt and then only occasionally. Mick didn't pounce immediately but as the stupidity of the idea sunk home he didn't let-up, not for years afterwards. " Got any more bright ideas for the band?" he would say, once every six months or so, " like recording an L.P. of waltzes, for instance?"

He would jump on all spurious attitudes with tigerish speed and I regarded this critical scrutiny as beneficial if hardly enjoyable. Not that Mick's assaults were selflessly directed for the benefit of his victims. That wasn't uppermost in his mind. Quite the contrary.

Nor was he less scathing about insincere praise. The band occasionally found themselves on the peripheries of show-biz—a short variety tour or on a mixed bill Sunday concert, when a singer or comic would bounce up to them with transparently phoney affirmation of goodwill.

" Great, boy! Just great! Loved it!" It was unlikely that the flatterer liked the band at all, especially if they had received a better ovation, but in back-scratching show-biz such laudatory remarks are part of an obligatory ritual.

Mick dealt with these spurious compliments in a manner that was lethally effective. It would be some time before the recipient was wondering what had hit him. He had a quite frightening analytical approach and I learned not to attempt any pretence with him.

We used to spend some time on the telephone (usually fairly early in the morning when he was sober) talking business and gossiping about people in the jazz world. Our observations were usually uncomplimentary. Indeed the pleasure of praising people is over and done with in a sentence or two but criticism can be spread out at length. The former may be a more Christian ethic but where is the fun?

I had no illusions that I would be similarly torn apart by

Mick if I became the subject of conversation with others and I had only to wait until the same afternoon, after he'd had a few drinks, to hear his views about me direct. Mostly, the expression of these sentiments was garbled, but the meanings were always patently clear.

He had an infuriating and, to me, expensive habit of phoning from the provinces and reversing the charges, usually when he was drunk, which was often, and usually to have a go at me.

Early one morning I received one of these reverse charge calls and immediately reacted in a hostile manner. It was well before the hour that Mick normally stirred and I thought I was in for one of his diatribes after a night on the booze. According to Melly in *Owning Up* I could be heard "barking" at some distance. I was, until I realized that it was a genuine call telling me the coach had been involved in a crash (this was before Appleby's time) and that vocaliste Jo Lennard was seriously ill. I had to cancel the band's engagements for the following week, but one promoter in the North insisted on settlement for the cost of advertising.

Believing, as I do, that the devil looks after his own, few of his children could be more favoured than Mick. It was incredible how, generally speaking, he used to fall on his feet. Opportunities seemed to open up, just for him. Much earlier the band appeared at a concert at the Trocadero, Elephant and Castle, before an audience of what, on that side of the Thames, George Melly would have described as "transpontines". Mick, an inveterate joke-teller, was host to a yarn about a certain person who had just been convicted of offences against boy scouts. Mick was wondering how he could slip in the joke, when one of the "transpontines" shouted out a reference to Mick's relatively long hair, something associated in those days with Wildean immorality, and yelled out the convicted person's name.

"Funny you should mention him," said Mick. "I've just been reading a book of his. It's called *The Last of the Windjammers*." The hall erupted with combustible laughter and the band couldn't put a foot wrong for the rest of the show.

The devil was always by his side even when it appeared otherwise. He was at a party when an acquaintance introduced his girlfriend. The girl, making polite conversation, said, " I remember something about you." Mick, well drunk, pulled out his cock and asked if that organ would refresh her memory. " Oh, no," she replied, " I would have remembered one as small as that." Typically, it wasn't Mick that got into trouble with the boyfriend. It was the girl. She was berated by the man for knowing more about men's cocks than she ought.

Everyone is unique. Mick was just that bit more unique than most. A rake-hell with a high standard of social and financial honesty; the rebel who was the High Tory; a charmer with little conscience; a funny man who could be an intolerable bore if too deep in his cups. He was generosity and meanness in disparate parts and never consistent in either; very cruel to those whom he was, also, a good friend—there was every contradiction in the make-up of this memorable rascal.

The band's repertoire and performance had a familiar sameness over the years, but they made records showing their potential and, sometimes, their better points.

Mick, on form, was a trumpeter with a considerable range. Ian's clarinet I've always admired for its flowing ensemble line and sweet, singing tone. The rhythm section, *sans* banjo, was light and springy, Pete Appleby the pivot. They were not just another trad band.

With Mick's inherent gifts as a trumpeter, George's *bravura* posturings, and more rehearsals, the band could have been a lot more successful. As it was their impact was more social than musical.

One E.P. they made had the sly title " Young and Healthy " and very droll indeed was the picture on the sleeve. It was of Mick, clad only in gym shorts and slippers astride a vaulting horse.

Mick disbanded in 1961. I doubt if the band would have survived the hefty knocks the jazz business was shortly to receive but, in any case, he'd had enough of touring. It's an arduous way of earning a living and it would be difficult to assess how many thousands of miles the band had travelled.

He became, of all things, a grocer, in a Hooray county town in Sussex. He shook up a few of the inhabitants in this sprauncy neighbourhood but the charm still worked, his particular chemistry still had its effect.

A friend of mine, trombonist, Mike Collier, arranged to meet Mick at a pub in this town. Mick was late in arriving, of course, and Mike, surveying the customers, was riveted by the comments of a typical 'county' inhabitant. He was in his early 'fifties. He was wearing cavalry twill trousers, a blue blazer with a regimental badge resplendent on the breast pocket, a check shirt and spotted silk cravat, sported a military moustache and a fine line in Hooray chat. He was against Communists, immigrants, the Labour Party and Trade Unions. He advocated a strong line with strikers putting the country to ransom and had a few searing comments to make about unwashed, long-haired beatniks.

Mick eventually arrived, unkempt, rather drunk, and in need of a haircut. "Hello, Mickie, old boy," said the archetypal Hooray. "How bloody naice to see you. What are you feckin' well goin' to hev?"

Mick had obviously got them at it. I doubt if the Hooray talked in this fashion before Mick descended on the town.

He no longer follows any kind of occupation. He had a windfall; the devil smiled on him again. His ideal of doing nothing in the way of work—work and Mick were always uncomfortable bedmates—is now completely fulfilled.

I owe him quite a lot. Not for keeping me as his agent—I'm not at all sure that was a good thing—but for knocking a lot of affectations out of me—in the purely figurative sense for, miraculously, we never actually came to blows.

9

MAINSTREAM

The term 'Mainstream' as applied to jazz was first used by critic Stanley Dance who produced many records in the United States under this heading.

It applied to 'middle-period' jazz lying chronologically and generically between New Orleans and Be-bop, and the mainstream cult returned to their proper status many great American musicians who had been rather overlooked in the twin upsurge of revivalism and modern jazz.

Dance's "mistrust of a return to original simplicities", an opinion expressed in 1945 was, in the late 'fifties, shared by many British musicians who had once passionately embraced those simplicities. These "renegade traditionalists", as Humphrey Lyttelton described them, were the playing strength of mainstream with Lyttelton the principal renegade. It was ironic that the man largely responsible for the popularity of traditional jazz should have been the pace-setter. Humph has made a few twists and turns in his musical policies but always out of genuine conviction. He was undoubtedly converted to classic New Orleans jazz by his association with George Webb, a conversion that dominated his policy in his early days as a bandleader.

In the 'Blue Posts' one night he interrupted me—Humph was a great talker, the occasional, reluctant listener—to enthuse about the "warmth" of the wood-blocks to be heard on King Oliver's Creole Jazz Band recordings but he was soon using instrumentation not previously associated with jazz, including bongos, and asserted in one of his Club news-letters, January 1952, that he "preferred bongos to wood-blocks any day".

At my instigation he had a big band collaboration with Graeme Bell's band and soon after dropped the clanking banjo in favour of the guitar and *then* dropped the trombone *and* included the alto saxophone. The last was the ultimate heresy!

No banjo, no trombone, and a saxophone! To many hide-bound purists he was deserting 'true jazz' and going 'commercial'.

Quite the contrary. He was departing from a policy that could have made him a lot of money in the trad boom that was then gathering momentum. He probably thought his public would go along with him, but when they didn't he stuck to his guns. He played as he pleased.

In his news-letters and writing for the musical press he was in a good position to justify any changes in direction or criteria, although some of us rather got the impression he would go to almost any lengths to prove his infallibility. Indeed, if Humph were to stand on his head in Oxford Street in a rush hour he would surely essay an elaborate case for the exercise.

He could certainly go out on a limb. In his band's early days trombonist Harry Brown wasn't always able to obtain leave from the R.A.F. and Humph elected to appear without a trombonist rather than use someone who didn't match his requirements. The absence of a trombone in Humph's 'purist' days didn't then disturb his followers. For example, he packed the Liverpool Empire, a theatre of over 2,000 capacity, with himself, Wally Fawkes and a rhythm section. In those days, Humph was King.

At the Leicester Square Jazz Club he rebutted 'sitters-in' (musicians, including trombonists, who wanted to play a number or two with the band) and upset some with his refusals. Aware of this he made an announcement to the effect that even if the great U.S. trombonist Jack Teagarden were to walk through the door of the club he wouldn't wish him to sit in. Maybe this extraordinary announcement was meant to mollify the rejected, but it fell harshly on the ears of many.

When Duke Ellington's band came to this country in 1956, many devout Ellington worshippers, myself included, were grievously disappointed by the choice of programme and expressed our regrets. Lyttelton, writing in the *Melody Maker*, actually threatened physical violence if he personally heard any of these criticisms.

I wrote in reply : " Ellington, like Lyttelton, even, is a fallible being and can make mistakes in programme planning, could have listened to suspect advice or not taken any advice at all. All this is sad enough, but even sadder is that the articulate and influential Lyttelton should demand uncomplaining acceptance or he'll thump you one." The *Melody Maker* jokily added a rider that perhaps boxing promoter Jack Solomons would stage a Lyttelton-Godbolt fight. As Humph was six feet five and weighed about sixteen stone, it would have been an unequal, if hilarious, contest.

This wasn't the only occasion that Lyttelton threatened violence. In his book *Second Chorus* he asserted that " if anyone complained that he was going ' commercial ' I shall probably let them have it—right between the eyes."

Hostility to his critics on this score was quite understandable. It was hard enough to pursue a musical policy out of genuine conviction for less money when he could have easily have been riding on a lucrative bandwaggon without having these slurs on his artistic integrity.

In 1958 his departure from the traditional instrumentation was to reach its furthest point with an eight-piece band comprising himself, trombone, four saxophones and a rhythm team. It was a highly musical and swinging band but very expensive to run. Furthermore, the trad idols, Barber, Bilk and Ball, had overtaken him in popularity. He was no longer King.

British jazz owes much to this untypical character. He is an intelligent, witty and articulate spokesman for the music and not only for the kind he plays. He has been a dignified figure in the British scene. Jazz doesn't need dignifying, but it comes of no harm in having such a spokesman and exponent and although his social background helped to give him publicity, it wasn't only this that made him a significant figure.

" The Autocrat on the Bandstand " was the heading for one early article about him, and I quote from another : " He has the well-bred Englishman's calm and confidence in his place in the world. Combine this with a healthy egotism and his ability to support it and the result is a young man on whom the petty irritations of life leave little impression."

This was written of him in *News Review*, article unsigned, in 1950. The piece continues: "His outspokenness is a source of apprehension in jazz circles and for good reason. During a recent B.B.C. Jazz Club quizz broadcast, the interrogator attempted to jog Humphrey's memory by writing a name on a slip of paper. Humph observed this stratagem and denounced it loud and clear over the air."

That was very characteristic of Lyttelton, but I wouldn't agree that petty irritations left him unmoved. Quite a number of things, and people, irritated him, particularly critics.

This kind of hostility isn't, of course, restricted to jazz musicians. There was the tart observation by Sibelius, I think, that he couldn't recall having seen any statues erected in honour of critics and the classic jazzman's barb against the species has been attributed to the American bandleader, Eddie Condon. Told that the French jazz pundit, Hughes Panassie, was critical of his records Condon said, " How come these French cats are telling us how to play jazz? Do I tell Panassie how to jump on a grape?"

There was the delightful occasion when the well-bred Englishman slaughtered a cocky American critic with just one word. The American was Ralph Berton, brother of Vic, a drummer famous in the 'twenties. Berton was given to purple prose but, on a B.B.C. " Jazz Brains Trust " with Humph also on the panel, he affected the persona of the intellectual beatnik and jettisoned his usual high-flown verbiage in favour of Runyonesque slang.

Humph made his comment and smart-Alec Berton breezily asked, " Say, Humphrey, old boy, what kind of language is that?"

Humph fixed him with a characteristic fish-eye and the peremptory, crushing reply, delivered in his well-bred accent, was, " *English* ".

Humph has a marvellous speaking voice with none of the irritating over-articulation of his class. Its resonances were well suited to this brief and crushing riposte.

Although Humph delighted in trouncing critics, this didn't

deter him from becoming one, writing regularly for the musical papers. The "unstudied confidence and healthy ego" permeated his writing although whatever the tone or tenor of his sentiments, he was never anything less than highly readable. He could easily have made a career out of journalism alone, or as a cartoonist.

In one of his monthly news-letters to his club members, he attacked the *Melody Maker* for quoting him out of context. The *Melody Maker*, tongue in cheek, replied, " We forgot that when a man reaches a certain eminence he becomes qualified to lambast the press."

It wasn't only the press that Lyttelton lambasted. He has directed his fire-power against the B.B.C. promoters, managers, agents (of course) and even some musicians who have worked for him. He has never been one to court friendship from those who have publicized him, employed him or worked for him. He's very much his own man.

Personally, I have enjoyed following him rampaging through the business and even though I have had the lash of his tongue, I have agreed with most of his pronouncements, not that it would bother him too much if it were otherwise.

Some professional musicians gunned for him. Jack Bentley, one-time dance band trombonist, now writing a show-biz column in the *Sunday Mirror*, wrote of Humph in the *Musical Express*, in 1951 : " It is high time that someone exploded the Humphrey Lyttelton myth. Lyttelton starts off with a distinct handicap. His ideas are prolific but a limited technique strangles them from birth ". In another review in the same paper Bentley jibed that " Humph had a ' cracking ' good time on a certain broadcast," referring to Lyttelton's cracked notes.

These allegations were not entirely without foundation. Humph often used to try and play outside his range and I certainly don't deny the importance of technique, but in one chorus he could express more jazz truths than most of the dance band musicians-cum-jazzmen would in a lifetime's blowing.

These criticisms were motivated by a degree of envy. Most of the professionals had come up the hard way and objected to the extra-musical publicity Lyttelton had received on account of his upper-crust background.

Moreover, the more jazz-minded of them were compelled to spend the best part of their working hours grinding out ordinary dance music. The title of Humph's first book, *I Play As I Please*, crystallized the difference between their respective positions. *I Play As I Please* and *Second Chorus* by Humph should be in every jazz-lover's library. Both are unique documents, and very readable. In *Second Chorus* he is extremely funny about people asking him if his uncle, Capt. Oliver Lyttelton, then Colonial Secretary, later Lord Chandos, approved of his atypical activities.

" They never ask me," he wrote, " if I approve of his."

He mentions his social background in the same book asserting that if it would help him to fulfil a long-cherished ambition to take his band to America, he would gladly go out and buy a monocle. He didn't have to. The band toured America with great success without the help of the single eye-glass, once the mark of a nob.

During my term as an agent and club promoter, I booked Humph and his band scores of times and he never gave less than superb value as an *entertainer* whether playing trumpet or clarinet, singing or announcing, not to mention occasional forays on the drums and the piano, although in the late 'sixties, he left his customers more stimulated than satisfied when many of his sidemen, young modernists, were seemingly at stylistic variance with the leader. Here his technical limitations were revealed as he attempted to keep pace with the young Turks he deliberately gathered around him.

Humph's adventurousness in moving away from the trad stereotype was poorly received by the B.B.C. A senior producer told me, with querulous petulance, " Lyttelton may play as he pleases but what he plays doesn't please me ", a striking case of the pigmy bemoaning the giant.

This was because news of the trad boom had penetrated those mysterious regions in Broadcasting House where the planners lay cocooned, and instructions were issued to producers that the banjos were to ring out on their programmes. Jazz has always been Cinderella to ' Auntie ', but she warmly embraced trad—until it declined in popularity, and the amount of time she devotes to jazz has become once again minimal.

My appreciation of Lyttelton's talents and influences is not written under any obligation to an Old Pals' Act. Despite my knowing him in the George Webb days, being in nominal partnership with him and Lyn Dutton and repeatedly booking him over the years, I can't recall more than half a dozen somewhat one-sided conversations with him. A rather aloof man he would, I think, have often preferred to be otherwise. But it wasn't in him to unbend. I think his physical height and social conditioning had much to do with this. On the other hand although he enjoyed praise and recognition, he patently took the view that the price of admission to a club or dance hall didn't automatically include command of his ears.

It was easy to tell when Humph was disinclined to converse. You were met with his non-smiling smile. He's a man whom I've admired more than I liked.

The last time I saw him was at 100 Oxford Street. We briefly discussed a pre-war film of bandleader Jack Payne hilariously ' conducting' an even more hilarious arrangement of ' Tiger Rag' at the Paris Olympia. Humph told me that Louis Armstrong, then also in Paris, attempted to join the proceedings but was rebutted by Payne.

It occurred to me that Jack Teagarden would have suffered a similar rebuttal had he tried to sit in with Humph's Band at the Leicester Square Jazz Club in 1949 but I didn't make the comment. Not that I was given much chance. I was about to make a contribution to the conversation when Humph's head slowly turned to an angle of about ninety degrees. This gesture of his wasn't new to me and I moved away. Looking back, I saw that his head was still turned : he had obviously overestimated the time it would take me to go away.

I genuinely welcomed the mainstream phase. Even during my most enthusiastic support for revivalism I hadn't jettisoned those records and tastes I had acquired as a collector years before—records of the big bands with whom most of the American mainstreamers ' paid their dues', as well as white players like Bix Beiderbecke, Jack Teagarden and Pee-Wee Russell—not to mention a few less fashionable names cast in the critical ditch in the ideological upheavals of the 'forties.

I became known as the mainstream agent, representing Bruce Turner and his Jump Band, the Fairweather-Brown All-Stars, Wally Fawkes' Troglodytes, the Tony Coe Quintet and Fat John and his Band.

As an agent, monetary considerations were, of necessity, uppermost in my mind but I enjoyed representing these bands. I had pride in my products . . . and quite a few problems.

Although the mainstreamers had rejected trad, they survived only in trad clubs. Apart from the ' Six Bells ' in Chelsea there were no venues devoted to the style—an odd situation, because mainstream wasn't harmonically or rhythmically such a drastic departure from trad. In fact some cynics dubbed it " trad without the banjo " or " modern without the technique ", but with its wider repertoire, more extensive use of arrangements, inclusion of the saxophone in the instrumentation and banjo-less rhythm sections it was just that much non-conformist to make bookings hard to come by—a situation to which I was no stranger.

There were many liberal-minded enthusiasts who saw jazz as a spectrum where one could take one's choice of colour. This was an agreeable ideal but, in the hard realities of band-booking promoters and agents, one had to be acutely aware of stylistic classifications. Bread and butter and sometimes a little jam were involved.

Many promoters had the strongest antipathy towards mainstream. Understandably these played safe with the banjo bands, although I didn't always take such a reasonable view of their attitude. In fact I used to upbraid them for not appreciating the *quality* I was offering. It was an utterly illogical attitude. Those businessmen were not obliged to take the bands their customers didn't want.

But mainstream attracted a degree of critical acclaim and a vociferous minority support as purist and righteous in their convictions as any revivalist. Slowly, I managed to nudge the bands into clubs and obtain the occasional broadcast. Mainstream jazz obtained a foothold in the business.

Wally Fawkes' Band included, at various times, four players who had been active in jazz before the war : Lennie Felix, a pianist of *bravura* in the Fats Waller-Earl Hines tradition, Dave

Wilkins, a West Indian trumpeter who had played with Fats Waller and Ted Heath, Russ Allen, bassist with many nightclub bands, and trumpeter Ian 'Spike' Mackintosh.

Jazz has been a magnet to an extraordinary variety of people, but few as rare as Spike, timber merchant and part-time jazzman. Short, dapper, urbane, plummy in accent and then in his forties, he was an extremely generous and friendly character but had, nevertheless, the most colossal cheek, imperiously knocking up hotels and garages in the early hours of the morning demanding drinks, food or petrol.

In the nocturnal hours he would descend on friends with an armful of 78 rpm records, mostly by Louis Armstrong, and insist on playing them at the loudest possible volume and singing (*à la* Louis Armstrong) the choruses throughout the records, utterly oblivious of any neighbours' reactions to the sound of Louis and disciple at maximum volume so late at night. If the usually unwilling host acquiesced, Spike would be playing records until the dawn chorus joined in. His night's enjoyment over, he would drive home, freshen up and be at his office sharp at 9.30 a.m. as neat and dapper as any city businessman should look. He maintained a punishing raver's life-style well into his fifties. He had, of necessity, an iron constitution.

Although we were the best of friends we used to have a few sharp exchanges. "A council schoolboy with a chip on his shoulder" was one of his retorts after I had complained about the behaviour of some of his city friends, some of whom, I can say quite unequivocally, were the nastiest individuals it has ever been my misfortune to encounter.

"Judge a man by his friends" is the adage, but this didn't apply to the charming and genial Spike but, almost without exception his mates were a remarkable tally of bores, buffoons and bullies.

He once claimed that he was "broke". In my characteristic manner I remarked that living in fashionable Cuffley, owning a large car and having his sons at public school hardly added up to living on the bread-line, or maybe he was broke because of these luxuries. Spike was furious, not, apparently, at the prospect of living in a little semi-detached or using public transport even, but the thought of the Mackintosh off-spring

not attending public school aroused him to apoplectic fury. " Do
you expect me to send my sons to a COUNCIL school?" he
spluttered in shocked disbelief. He was genuinely alarmed at
the prospect.

I was with Spike at a party given by Wally, a very generous
host. There was a lot of drinking. Spike fell against a bamboo
screen bringing down the various *objets d'art* arrayed on the
ledges. The noise awakened Wally's eldest daughter, Joanna,
then about six years old, and she stood, in tears, at the top of
the stairs that led directly into the drawing-room. It was well
after midnight. Spike, sprawled at the bottom of the screen, with
bits of Italian glassware and sprays of potted creeper trailing from
his head, looked up, saw Joanna and enquired, " I know it's
none of my business, Wally, but shouldn't that child be in bed?"

But it was me, not Spike, who was savaged by Wally's then
wife, Sandy. Apparently I had not shown any concern for
Joanna's distress and Sandy tore into me. Not a word to Spike,
who was now on his feet and looking for his glass. It was one of
those occasions when the maxim " sometimes you can't win "
crossed my mind.

When Spike and Mick Mulligan talked politics they were in
complete agreement. Both were rank Tories with the unshake-
able belief that their party had the divine right to rule. Neither
could pursue a discussion with an opponent of this philosophy,
but when the arguments arose such phrases as " it's the training
that matters " and " some are born to lead " were repetitively
paraded and whilst these profound political tenets were being
expounded the drinks would go down as if there were no tomorrow.

But there was one occasion when Ian rounded on Mick. It
was at the Cottage Club in Litchfield Street, off Charing Cross
Road, then a jazzman's meeting place. Ian, Max Jones, Mick
and myself were discussing the various trumpeters Duke Ellington
had used in his bands and how it was sometimes difficult to
establish their identity.

Mick was mainly silent, but eventually offered an opinion.

Mackintosh scoffed, " Oh, for God's sake, Mick. Don't talk
such rot. It was obviously Cootie Williams on that version.
Bloody hell, man, you sound just like a day boy!"

H

On occasions Spike's trumpet playing was exceptionally good, his lead strong and propulsive with a big round tone, very much in the Armstrong manner, but on his off nights he played so raggedly that the band sagged with him. I was often in a state of fearful suspense as to what form Spike would be in. He had a considerable talent which he never quite fulfilled, mainly because of his fondness for a drop.

After twelve months or so Wally broke up the band. He said, " I'm a believer in quitting at the bottom."

Bruce Turner had established a reputation on clarinet and alto saxophone with Freddy Randall and Humphrey Lyttelton. He had considerable prowess on the latter instrument, not always appreciated. It was an instrument with all other saxophones long regarded with hostility on ideological grounds by some factions of the jazz fraternity. When Bruce made his debut at the Birmingham Town Hall with the Humph Band a demented few in the audience displayed a banner with the words—apropos the hated saxophone—" GO HOME DIRTY BOPPER ". George Melly succinctly wrote of the incident: " To execute this project reveals a fanaticism verging on the unbalanced." How true!

Surprisingly Bruce formed his own band. Surprising, as Bruce was a vague and diffident individual not, it was thought, suited to the tribulations and hazards of bandleading. Bruce's apparent distance from the realities of life were revealed at Gloucester Place when he bought a second-hand motor car. It soon broke down and he was asked why he didn't take along someone who knew about motor cars when he made the purchase. Bruce replied, " But, Dad, the guy who sold it to me knew all about motor cars."

He was an unexpected success as a bandleader. No disciplinarian, he commanded respect for the quality of his playing and he imposed a recognizable stamp of his band's style. A vegetarian, non-smoker and teetotaller, he was, however, a massive, compulsive eater of confectionery. For him to devour several Mars Bars in quick succession wasn't uncommon. He never bought anyone a drink, not even a promoter or dance hall manager who might have been more favourably disposed to the band had

with arms linked as Coe and his fellow gods comfortably made their way to the bar. In respect of nicotine and alcohol Tony differed from Bruce.

John Cox (Fat John) was small and chubby, but hardly a bundle of joy. A modernist, he had, for the money, been a reluctant drummer with Mick Mulligan. He bore playing ' Dixieland ' with fortitude if not without complaint. John's complaints were unceasing. The day had no pleasure for him unless there were reasons for bitter moans and if he couldn't find any reasons he would invent some.

When Mick's band folded John formed a band of highly talented musicians but it was far too ' modern ' for those clubs that were sparingly, grudgingly taking mainstream bands. The band folded and to this day the pianist snarls and grimaces when he sees me. The implacable hostility of this one has gone on for years. " You sold the band down the river," is his emotive accusation.

No agent deliberately " sells a band down the river ". Commission is his life blood and the more bands he has working the more commission he enjoys. Every successful band is another step forward. It can only enhance the agent's reputation prompting other bands to approach him for representation. But no agent can *make* promoters take bands they don't want. In John's case it was a great pity. He had a rare knack of discovering talented unknowns and the arrangements were highly musical.

John, despite his unceasing strictures, had a sharp sense of humour and we got on well. He was funny about the vagaries of bandleading. He told a cautionary tale about members of a band being unhappy with the leader and, wishing to depose him, one of them approached him with the chilling words, " Harry, me and the boys have been having a bit of a chat. . . ."

Clarinettist Sandy Brown and trumpeter Al Fairweather first played together in Edinburgh, their band based entirely on the classic Louis Armstrong Hot Five and Hot Seven records. They came to London and under Sandy's leadership were soon established as a significant contribution to the scene. They were no longer stylistically hidebound. Steve Race was wholly enthusiastic about them. In his *Melody Maker* series, " Great Records Of Our Time " he included Sandy's *McJazz*, the first British record to appear in the series.

Humphrey Lyttelton also praised them highly. Rightly so. It was one of the delights of the 'fifties to hear Al's trumpet lead; trim, spare and dry, the perfect foil for Sandy's often extravagant and dissonant leaps up and down the register of his instrument with a broad and muscular tone.

Sandy left to form his own band and Al asked me to represent him. It wasn't easy selling the new band. Again, it was a case of a former ' sideman ' who didn't have the drawing power of his former boss. But Sandy came back and under the name of the Fairweather-Brown All-Stars business picked up.

Al, a very good cartoonist, used to send me amusing drawings on the backs of envelopes when he settled his commission accounts—which he did with unfailing promptness. An agent will clearly remember an attribute as rare as this. These drawings were little cameos about the business. He had a hilarious cartoon published in the *Melody Maker*. It represented the various phases of a jazz musician's life commencing as an eager enthusiast listening to records and ending up as a jaded touring musician. It was a gem that contained so many truths.

Unfortunately, there were many tensions and disputations between us. Things would go wrong in a way that almost had me believing that some unseen and malevolent force was bedevilling our relationship. This feeling was quite irrational, but nevertheless very real. It was a pity because I liked Al very much. Apart from being a fine musician he was a very sincere and genuine person.

I was also very fond of Sandy, but he was a horse of quite a different colour. Unlike the quiet, self-effacing Al, Sandy was the loquacious egotist.

I once remarked to Sandy that had he and Al stuck to trad they could have made a lot of money. Sandy shuddered. " It wouldn't have been worth it," he said, and Al, who unlike Sandy, relied on the band for his living, was in full agreement.

Here were two examples of " renegade traditionalists " who knowingly forsook certain profit for their musical principles.

Since I completed this book Sandy has died at the tragically early age of forty-six. I heard the news over the radio. I felt acute shock and grief. I just couldn't believe that he had gone. I cried for a week. It was only then I realized how much he had entered my psyche, how much I regarded him. Death had to be the cruel reminder of his rare qualities as man and musician. Should he have looked down on my sorrow which, I confess, surprised me as much as it hurt, he would at least have been amused by my tears, for we never lost the opportunity to cut and thrust. This verbal duelling, sometimes extended to lengthy correspondence, was very much a part of our relationship. It got a trifle heated at times, but was never really unfriendly.

I entertained the famous negro trumpeter, Red Allen, one evening and Sandy was another guest. I didn't see or hear much of Red Allen. I heard and saw a lot of Sandy, though. He took over.

He liked a drink and he liked a word. This was an occasion when the combination was overwhelming. It was a long time before I forgave him his behaviour that night.

A few months before his death he gave an imitation of myself in an anti-social mood and although this was over the telephone I laughed heartily in genuine mirth, so accurate was the tone, the accent, the inflexions, the phraseology. It was the last time I ever spoke to him.

Sandy had not been so active musically over recent years and ironically, typically, his death had the fraternity rediscovering on records the surging vitality and lyrical expressiveness of his playing. He was undoubtedly one of the most original, if not *the* most original of British jazz talents as a player, composer and organizer of fine records that will assuredly stand the test of time.

When I re-read the critical references to Sandy in this book I wondered if, as a mark of respect, I should withdraw them but, again, had he been looking down he would, I'm certain, have disapproved of such excisions. Bowing to the unheard but distinct voice I have kept them in.

The mainstreamers had an influence in very unexpected quarters. The most colourful of the trad bandleaders, Acker

Bilk, decided on a policy embracing aspects of 'mainstream'. He dropped the banjo and looked around for suitable musicians to further this change of policy.

He instructed a booker in brother David's office, Frank Parr, to ring me to enquire the telephone numbers of Bruce Turner and his trumpet player Ray Crane. I sensed why Parr was making these enquiries, especially as he sounded so casual and gave no reason for the requests. Frank and I were not fond of each other and I thought this approach very, typically, cheeky.

In truth there was no reasonable objection to Acker directing his office staff to approach musicians but it was typical of Frank's gall to ring the agent of the players concerned, but I gave the numbers without comment although not, of course, without making an entry in my mental 'black book' which, by now, was a tome of considerable bulk. Ray Crane declined the offer, much to Frank's astonishment, but another trumpet player from 'my camp', Al Fairweather, joined instead.

Sometime later David Bilk, an individual with whom I had enjoyed a cut-and-thrust relationship invited me to attend a party given at one of the Czech Embassies in Highgate to launch the English tour of a Czech jazz band.

Frank was there, very drunk. He was seated, rigid, on the window-sill staring and blinking at a row of empty glasses. There must have been a sudden, dramatic awareness that these were the silent spokesmen of his problem and in one sweep he had the lot in the garden below.

Quickly, large Slav officials of the Embassy with padded shoulders and flared nostrils whisked him into another room. It was like a scene from an anti-Communist B film as the door slammed behind them. I almost expected to hear him screaming as the villainous Reds tortured him, although they would have been hard pressed to get any reaction from someone so completely anaesthetized.

This picture of Communist infamy was sustained by the spectacle of Frank sitting bolt upright in a chair and staring fixedly ahead as though drugged. He was, but only by hefty gulps of Slivovitz supplied by the generous hosts.

I was at the bar with Acker and David and, referring to my 'black book', I mentioned Frank's cheek in phoning me for telephone numbers, and jocularly expressed the opinion that had they been in pursuit of Sandy Brown, and managed to get him in the band as well as Bruce and Al, and Acker bought himself a baton and conducted, there might be the makings of a fair noise in the Bilk band.

Not a bad gag, I thought, considering that Sandy and Acker played the same instrument. Acker roared with laughter and David, forced into an awkward position by his brother's merriment, managed a cracked smile. David's reluctance to laugh was typical of the code that obtained at the Bilk office in Wardour Street, usually known as Mystery House: as its occupants were hardly ever at their desks, despite the number of grandiose schemes trumpeted from that source.

All would fiercely take up arms on the others' behalf, often in the face of indisputable truths and irrespective of private feelings. I frequently wondered if it was an oath they had to take before they went on the pay-roll.

When Bruce left the band, quite amicably, there was a variant of the " ' Go home, Dirty Bopper ' " theme, this time conceived by an idiotic promoter in South London. He booked Acker's band after Bruce's departure and displayed a poster with wording to the effect that without the odious saxophone the band was back to its normal, true (trad) character.

Not so. The impact of Bruce and Al has had a lasting effect.

IT'S POLO AT 'URLINGHAM

Clubs have been the jazz musician's spawning grounds and the social backbone of the movement. From the days of the pre-war rhythm clubs to post-war dancing to jazz clubs, it has flourished best in pubs and basements.

The revivalist and mainstream jazzmen liked playing for dancers. Movement on the floor generated atmosphere. There was little dancing at modern clubs. The modern jazzman took the view that his art was of a more cerebral nature and merited rapt and undivided attention.

The globe-trotting Graeme Bell Band introduced jazz for dancing at the Leicester Square Jazz Club in 1948 and later at the London Jazz Club and his own club. It was a policy enthusiastically endorsed by Humphrey Lyttelton. In the L.J.C. newsletter he slammed serious-minded purists.

" If we're going to be purists let's emulate New Orleans in just one respect. The dance halls in red-light Storyville district may have been unsavoury places but they were free from the species of cranky ' art form ' obsessionists who infest our jazz haunts over here. There was something prophetic about Buddy Bolden's* injunction ' to open up them windows and let the bad air out '. We have an atmosphere in this club which I believe to be just about perfect for the development of our music. Perfection will be attained when some of our more sedate authorities forget their dignity and get out on the floor. Jim Godbolt managed it, after all . . ."

To this day that rider has me puzzled. I can't ever recall

* A legendary New Orleans trumpeter who could be heard many miles distant.

claiming to be an authority and my contribution in the same
news-letter under the name of ' Odbot ' was slanted against the
pompous and over-serious but, as Humph's rider is almost tanta-
mount to praise, and this didn't fall too easily from his lips, I
acknowledge the compliment these twenty-seven years later.

From after the war and up to 1963 jazz clubs were formed
by the hundreds. Some, like the Nottingham, Redcar, Luton,
Reading and Wood Green clubs, the Mardi Gras, Liverpool, and
the Manchester Sports Guild enjoyed a long life, and the
premises with the longest jazz associations of all are 100 Oxford
Street, these first being used by the Feldman Swing Club as long
ago as 1942.

It is now run by Roger Horton, an engaging misanthrope
with a positive loathing for the British public. His was the heart-
felt cry, " Show me a banjo and you show me a profit " to which
he often added, apropos his pet aversion, " The British public
are a load of twots ! "

I have been associated with quite a few jazz club adventures
with varying success and have spent a few hundred anxious hours
waiting for the bodies to surge in. When they didn't it was a
miserable evening for all concerned. I lost money, the band lost
heart, and the few customers who had paid to come in wouldn't
be doing so the following week.

Sparse attendance is one sort of experience, but there is an
even more depressing one—the completely empty hall. Years
ago the Duke Ellington saxophonist Johnny Hodges recorded a
tuned called " Empty Ballroom Blues ". One night that title had
grim application as I stood at the door of a club with the space
between me and the bandstand devoid of a living soul.

It was at the Piccadilly Club, Denman Street, off Piccadilly
Circus. Initially I was the booking agent on behalf of a promoter
who had entered into an agreement with two archetypal Jewish
brothers who owned the premises. In the 'thirties it had been
a night club called the Vortex, owned by a Lady Torrington
and Steve Donoghue, the jockey, he of the once-famous catch
phrase, " Come on Steve ! " In those halcyon days it was notorious for bottle parties and catered for monocled toffs who attended
haunts like this for the vicarious pleasure of being present when

the police made a raid. There were no monocled toffs and be-furred ladies showing up at the Piccadilly Club in 1956, but we did get a raid, of a sort.

After the opening night the *Melody Maker* gave the club a favourable review. The reporter praised the atmosphere and Wally Fawkes' Band. He also reported that the "cadaverous" Jim Godbolt handled awkward situations like putting a ban on the bar at closing time with "great tact and jazz feeling". There can't be many people in the entertainment business who have put up the bar with true "jazz feeling" and that compli-ment was about the only satisfaction I got from this disastrous venture.

The opening night was a great success. Opening nights usually are. Some come along out of curiosity, the practised free-loaders throng the bar and the bandleaders turn up to get their faces in the photographs. But a successful opening night is no true indication of business to come. The promoter, sensing disaster, quit after the first few nights leaving the brothers morosely listening to a music they didn't like.

I took over the erstwhile promoter's responsibilities with the naïve belief that as we were offering something different we must eventually succeed. The *policy* difference between the Piccadilly Club and every other jazz club in London was that our premises were licensed and served hot meals. The *essential* difference between our club and others soon crystallized. They were doing the business and we were not.

Every night the brothers, myself and odd well-wishers would conduct a mournful post-mortem. It became a ritual. One night there was a knock on the door and we quickly put the glasses out of sight. Two scruffy men gained admission on some pretext and I sensed they were policemen. They hinted they were thirsty. "Like a nice cup of tea, bhoys?" asked the elder brother, nervously puffing at a cheroot. He, too, had sensed trouble. Vaguely, I thought I had seen one of them in a situation outside the normal policeman's beat, although still not certain they were coppers. I probed. "Haven't we met somewhere before?" I asked, casually. His reply was non-committal, but it gave me the answer. "Was it in Earl's Court?" he said. It was, but, strictly speaking, we had not met until this night.

A couple of years before, Mick Mulligan rang me up one afternoon and asked me if I would like "to go to the flicks" with him. I was taken aback. Mick rarely went to the cinema and I was puzzled why he was asking me to accompany him. He archly explained this was a special screening at a flat in Earl's Court for a special price of thirty shillings. I still didn't comprehend.

"Of course," said Mick in mock-pained tones, "if you don't want to come to the pictures with me, or you're washing your hair . . ."

That special showing was the only blue film session I have ever attended. When Mick, George Melly and myself arrived, Mick pointed to the hall sofa strewn with umbrellas, brief cases and bowler hats. The impresario, a City gent, had no problem in finding customers from the panelled sanctums of the banks, insurance companies and stockbrokers in the respectable square mile.

A group of well-dressed, middle-class men of varying ages stood giggling in a corner of the room. The impresario, eager to induce the right mood for the delights to come, was telling them a naughty joke. A sheet had been rigged up to act as a screen and the cinematograph operators, two gentlemen not long off another sort of duty, arrived. Their Oxford-blue shirts, dark blue ties, dark blue serge trousers and heavy boots indicated a calling where access to films of this nature was easier for them than it was to the rest of us. The senior operator mounted a box and fiddled with apparatus. "Right, Gents. Ready for the show? 'Arry, 'and me the lesbian lot, will yer? Ta. Now this will get you going, gents. There's some right little darlings amongst this team, I can tell yer."

A lesbian orgy was the beginning of a string of technically crude, quite hilarious pornographic films. They had been made on extremely cramped budgets. One had a particularly thin story line. It consisted of a gentleman walking through a corn field where he conveniently encountered a nude and obliging female. In another epic the casting director had obviously been hard pushed to fill the roles satisfactorily. The leading man, middle-aged and paunchy, had trouble in maintaining an erection, an unfortunate failing in a production of this kind, and one on which the camera cruelly lingered, perhaps in hope of a revival. Perhaps he had exhausted himself at rehearsals. Whatever, we hooted with laughter when the leading lady seized the organ with both hands and furiously jerked it up and down in the manner of a native woman using a pestle to pound maize in a kraal but, alas, to no avail. There was a merciful ' fade '. In another production the undeniable athleticism of two men and a girl compensated for the aesthetic limitations of the theme and the quite gruesome ugliness of the participants. Again, it appeared that the casting director's lot had been a difficult one.

The interlocutory remarks of the senior operator—he was genuinely enthusiastic about his wares—nearly prompted one of the belly-laughter explosions that Mick and I used to have. It was a struggle to contain ourselves. The impresario, a thoroughly gross individual, was put out that we laughed at all. This was a serious porn show, not an occasion for hilarity. We could have been equally put out that the supply of light ale was limited to one bottle per man. Not that we needed drink. The programme was intoxicating enough.

" Well, gentlemen," said the chief operator after an hour or so, " We're now coming to the P.C. de resistant—isn't that right, 'Arry?"

Harry nodded energetically and twisted glottal noises came from Mick's direction.

At this point Mick, George and myself left. Mick had a broadcast. This was one category of engagement for which Mick was never late or drunk, probably because he knew there would be no more broadcasts if he was either. This strict rule wasn't broken even for the " P.C. de resistant " of this extraordinary thirty shillings' worth.

Here, at the Piccadilly Club, was the chief operator of the Earl's Court blue film show and still he had not declared himself as a police officer. I eventually drew him out by complimenting him on his apparent knowledge of licensing laws and enquired how it was he knew so much. He smirked, looked at his mate and said, " Shall we tell them?" His mate smirked, and nodded. The chief operator produced his card.

" Like a nice cup of tea, bhoys?" said the elder brother, now puffing at his cheroot more nervously than ever. Perhaps the officers came looking for extra-curricular business. If so, they were unlucky and they got no more than a cup of tea.

When things go wrong and business is bad, tempers get frayed. There can't be many people with whom Wally Fawkes had quarrelled but I was one of them and after a brief argument he strode out of the club in high fury.

On another occasion Mick and I had one of our periodic disputes and he gave me the sack, again. He kept repeating, " It's all down to swallows then. All right? All down to swallows, then?" After he had repeated this about ten times I wearily assented. The following morning I rang him to enquire when we could meet and clear up outstanding business before he went to another office and Mick could barely remember a word of the altercation. I was immensely relieved. After the losses at this club I needed Mick's commission.

The club carried on for a few months and occasionally Spike Mackintosh brought along some of his City mates. I got to fear these visits, not because of Spike, but because of his quite wretched friends. God in heaven above! They were the ultimate in nastiness and, as it happens, extreme right-wing reactionaries to a man.

The club eventually folded and the brothers went into partnership with two young men who turned the premises into a strip club. I went to the refurbished premises one night to sort out finances with the brothers. The club room had been decorated in garish, pseudo-Moorish fashion—" Like a Jewish Taj Mahal " was Wally's description when he popped in to see the transformation.

At the younger brother's firm insistence I stopped to watch the show. It was fortunate that Mick wasn't present or there might have been an eruption of hysterical laughter at the spectacle of rain-coated gentlemen scampering to occupy the front seats as they became vacant, and at the finale of the show when a young lady, almost naked, walked down the plinth in the centre aisle with all heads turned for the final divestment.

Arriving at the end of the plinth she revealed all, but modesty quickly returned and she closed the act by putting her hand over the orifice only momentarily revealed.

" Luvly show, isn't it, Jimmy bhoy?" said the elder brother.

" Yes," added the younger. " It's got real class," and I thought of all those bleak nights when jazz bands played to only a handful of people. I was in the wrong business. Females stripping off attracted a lot more customers than jazz music but my rationale for failure was that our drinking and dining jazz club was ahead of its time.

Previously, I had tried to obtain premises in the West End by following up an advertisement in the *Melody Maker*. I telephoned the number and a very grand-voiced gentleman answered. Although attitudes to jazz—this was about 1954—were becoming more favourable, I was still cautious about specifically mentioning that I wanted the premises for a jazz club. But he guessed.

" If it's a *jess* club you're wanting it for, Mr Godbolt, the *ensah* is *noah*, *Aive* turned down *quate* a few who want the premises for *thet*. *Aive* got a nice place *heah* and a staff of waiters in white coats and *Ai'm* looking for a *darnce* club with a *naice clientele*. *Aive* nothing against them but I don't want any darkies kicking a gong around and boogy-woogying about *mai* place."

This is a verbatim report of his comments. I had the feeling he wasn't my man, even if I had a ready clientele of ' gong-kicking, boogy-woogying darkies ' to occupy the attention of his white-coated waiters.

Wally Fawkes discovered the room at the ' Six Bells ' and suggested that I approached the brewers with a view to hiring it for a jazz club.

We opened on Monday evenings with his band and for several weeks played to only a handful of people, but one Monday evening an unexpected group of forty people arrived. They were members of the Inter-Varsity Club and their secretary, Clive Chester, was a jazz enthusiast. They transformed the atmosphere and the tenor of business. The old adage that people attract people was never more clearly, pleasurably, demonstrated.

The ' Six Bells ' already had an honourable place in British jazz history. The writer and composer, Spike Hughes, led a

Al Fairweather and Sandy Brown *(Photo : Melody Maker)*

Tony Coe
(Photo : T. A. Cryer)

Wally Fawkes
(Photo : Norman Hiller)

The Swinging Blue Jeans, 1962. *Left to right:* Ralph Ellis, Norman Kuhkle, Ray Ennis, Les Braid. *(Photo: Elizabeth Walkiden)*

Screaming Lord Sutch congratulating the Rt Hon. (later Sir) Harold Wilson after unsuccessfully competing with him at Huyton, Lancashire in the 1966 General Election

pioneer recording for the jazz band called the Decadents (on account of them recording for the Decca label and, no doubt, for jazz's dubious associations) and they recorded at the Chenil Galleries, a few yards from the ' Six Bells '.

At the end of the sessions the Decadents would rush into the pub for refreshment, inspiring Hughes to write "Six Bells Stampede ".

Visiting U.S. jazzmen, Duke Ellington's Band, clarinettist Jimmy Dorsey and trumpeter Muggsy Spanier, also recorded at the Chenil Galleries and drank at the ' Six Bells ', and from these jazzmen of another generation it became in the late 'fifties and throughout the 'sixties a venue for Humphrey Lyttelton, Al Fairweather, Sandy Brown, Bruce Turner, Fat John, Tony Coe and Wally Fawkes.

Wally, a highly popular person, attracted many people who came along to see and talk to him, even if they were not particularly enthusiastic about the band. From the rich seam of characters in the jazz world Wally was one of the most engaging. He possessed an insouciant magnetism that drew people into his company. He was someone who seemed to achieve much without ever seeming to try very hard and attracting people was one of them.

When Humph joined George Webb's band in 1947 he and Wally became close friends. On the journey to Hawick, Humph got into a carriage, saw that Wally wasn't present and hastily retreated to seek him out. It hadn't taken him long to assess the rest of us. We were not on his wave-length. Fawkes was, in his quiet, steely way, a match for Lyttelton. Humph's respect for Wally was revealed, albeit unintentionally, one night at the ' Blue Posts '. The Lyttelton band were taking a rather lengthy interval and after manager Lyn Dutton's almost tearful pleading that they return to the club, Humph addressed his men.

" Right! Off we go! *Bray! Parker! Hopkinson! Picard! Turner!* Ready, Wal?"

I've known Wally longer than anyone in my association with jazz and for these odd thirty years we have had a meaningful

I

and genuine relationship, even if somewhat on the tense side as though each were wary that the other was going to pull the wrong verbal switch. Wally's geniality was the marshmallow covering the hard centre and he showed more than a hint of steel when aroused. If situations occurred that were not to his liking, he would jut his chin skywards and utter a prolonged MMMMMM, like a king stag warning off his rivals in a rutting herd. If ever he and Humph had a quarrel in their thirteen years' association, it must have been a silent battle of the giants, physically as well as figuratively—both are over six feet tall—with Humph looking over his shoulder and Wally gazing skywards, the problem, whatever it was, lying untended between them. Both were skilled in lifemanship and neither given to losing their cool unless really exasperated.

Wally was the master of the offhand barb, the seemingly innocuous thrust, the victim often feeling the pain some time after the lunge. He cured me of telling jokes. " My favourite joke," he murmured with a keening blandness, chin turned upwards, after I had completed a lengthy, unfunny and oft-repeated tale. Not that he always won. In the 'fifties his band was on a broadcast with trumpeter Eddie Calvert, who had a hit parade success with a lachrymal confection entitled " Oh Mine Papa " played in a sickly, braying style. In the dressing-room Calvert was extolling the virtues of trumpeter Harry James over Louis Armstrong.

Wally's rapier thrusts buckled against Calvert's armadillo coating. The latter once arrived at Humph's Club and without invitation or any intimation appeared from behind the bandstand halfway through a number and dramatically, ineffectually, nay, disastrously, joined in. Even Humph was too flabbergasted to give the irrepressible Eddie the brush-off.

Wally based many of his characters in his cartoon strip " Flook " from people in the jazz world. One of them was Len Bloggs, a snarling anti-social inverted snob with a chip on his shoulder. For some reason I was the inspiration for this disagreeable misanthrope.

So accurate was Wally's draughtsmanship I was recognized by total strangers as the model for Bloggs who, in one story, was a schoolmaster. A man I had never seen before in my life approached me in a pub in Earl's Court and asked me if I was a schoolmaster. The question came as no surprise. I explained the connection and the man returned to his friend highly delighted with himself for recognizing me, but I had extremely mixed feelings about this sort of recognition.

On another occasion, at a jazz concert in the Festival Hall, I was again hailed by a total stranger, this time by name. The stranger was Steve Voce, a jazz critic from Liverpool, who informed me that he knew who I was from reading ' Flook ' and seeing me at a jazz concert. He was proud of his smart deduction and I was a little icy in acknowledging the recognition.

Running a jazz club gave me an illuminating insight into what is quaintly described as ' human nature '. Most people didn't begrudge paying a mere five or six shillings to listen to the cream of the country's jazz musicians, but there were some to whom getting into a jazz club without paying was a cardinal principle. They wouldn't dream of entering a cinema or leaving a restaurant without paying, but jazz clubs involved a different morality. Why, I don't know, but it was one of the facts of a club promoter's life. Some of them would try any physical manoeuvre and exercise ingenious verbal ploys rather than pay for admission. I discovered that the musicians had an extraordinary number of friends willing to lend support—moral but not financial. My standard rejoinder, which never went down well with these mumpers, was that friendship for individuals on the bandstand was best expressed by paying to see them.

I discovered that there were scores of jazz correspondents from all over the United Kingdom. If one of them came from, say, a local paper in Westmorland, I was assured that a write-up in that organ about the club would have them flocking from the lakes into the King's Road the following week.

The number of people in the film industry who were intending to make a film of the club and wanted free admission to assess the possibilities gave the lie to the erroneous belief that the industry was on its last legs.

If a club promoter allowed one in for free there would soon

be many others claiming the privilege. Money, and one's reputation were at stake. If the band was on a percentage of the total receipts, and if the bandleader had been doing some head-counting, as was his right, and there appeared to be a discrepancy between his share and the number of people in the hall, unpleasantness could ensue.

One night a bandleader looked at the money paid to him by the man I had on the door, expressed utter disbelief that the amount was so small, accused this man of cheating and threw the cash into the air.

The cashier, a large man, was going to do the bandleader a serious injury. I had a hard time trying to convince the bandleader that the figure was just and accurate and a harder time restraining the cashier from pulverizing the bandleader, himself quite drunk and ready for battle.

At least to avoid situations like this I tried to extract payment from all who entered, but as we were situated in the King's Road some of the ' Chelsea Set ' would appear. ' The Set ' is an amorphous term, but it will suffice to describe some of the well-heeled arrogants of the area. These were mumpers of considerable expertise, and very cheeky with it.

" Oh, don't be such a silly little man," spluttered one outraged Hetty when I politely requested payment. I'm six feet tall, but the appellation was indicative of a social attitude rather than a reference to my height. " I know the band very well," she snarled. " They've been to *hundreds* of my parties! Now let me pass!" It was a most imperious demand.

Her escort was silent until I suggested she was very unpleasant. His contribution was straight from P. G. Wodehouse. " Oh, I say, look here. I shall jolly well have to ask you to take that back!" She eventually departed snarling malevolently about " a silly little man " and protesting she could " buy the place over and over again ". An odd claim to wealth from someone not prepared to pay a few shillings' admission price.

Generally we had little real trouble, although I quickly made the discovery that individuals in the more exalted professions didn't necessarily have a higher standard of behaviour. On the contrary. My problem people were actors, doctors and solicitors.

One actor, particularly. To him the world was a stage (he

actually declaimed that line to me one night) which he constantly
paraded and tediously so when drunk. There was a solicitor,
since struck off, who came along solely to conduct the band.
He was ferret-like, middle-aged and slightly demented. He had
a rival in Johnny the Conductor and one night the band had
the benefit of two maestri, each with his own interpretation of
tempi, nuance and rhythm.

Another pestiferous nuisance was a young solicitor from a
strait-laced provincial town where his behaviour, perforce, was
impeccable but he regarded this jazz club in the soft South as
a place where, assisted by copious draughts of bitter (which
didn't compare with the brews in his home town, of course) he
could shake off the weighty burdens of his legal problems. He
was called Legal Pete.

There was a young Scots journalist who, freed from the
crimping restraint of life across the Border, consistently got
drunk, gatecrashed parties and spewed over his unwilling hosts'
carpet. He was called Ewan McSpewan.

This young man endeared himself to me on our first meeting
by proffering, as a statement of fact, that all managers and agents
were crooks. Indeed the further you go north the more this
notion of an entrepreneur's infamy is held to be credible and
applying particularly to those wicked parasites in the South—
a hot-bed of infamy to which, it's reasonable to note, hordes
from the North are flocking week by week, many of them loudly
protesting the superiority of the *mores* and people in areas to
which, quite sensibly, they have no intention of returning.

To me, London born and bred, these protestations of regional
pride from those who have migrated south are very irritating.

I've always held a high regard for jazz musicians and got on
well with most, but they are notorious for their reluctance to start
playing and for stretching their intervals. Getting musicians to or
back on to the bandstand is a herculean task. If one is a friend
of the musicians concerned, even less notice is taken of one's
agitated pleading. The conversation piece would proceed on
familiar lines. The phraseology maybe changed from time to
time but the reaction and rationale was constant.

" Ernie, it's about time you started playing."

" Oh? Joe's just come down from fixing his kit and he says there's no-one up there."

" That's immaterial. The stipulated starting time is 7.45. It's now 8.10."

" There's no point in playing to an empty hall, man."

" By the time you've drifted up there, tuned up, and had a lengthy discussion as to what your first number will be the place will be half-full."

" Oh, very funny man. You do like your little joke, don't you? Look man, when the customers arrive we'll be up there, O.K.? You worry too much, man."

" I'm paid to worry and you've got your priorities mixed-up. The public decide what time they arrive and expect to see you on the bandstand playing your instruments anytime after the advertised start, which is about twenty minutes ago."

" O.K., man. Have it your way. I just love playing to an empty hall. Sort of inspires me! Another pint, please, Maisie. Now . . . where was I . . . oh yes . . . so I told this bird straight. Look here, darling, I said, there's plenty of chicks who want to know, I said . . ."

I must have appeared unduly fussy, querulous and pedantic, even, over this matter of punctuality. Having customers in the hall and the band drinking in the bar used to make me a little agitated.

It was implied, as a counter criticism, that I didn't understand how the creative mind ticked. I was reminded that I wasn't talking to bank clerks who have to be at their desks at fixed times, but to *musicians*—creative artistes.

The same creative artistes were, however, precise, attentive and pedantic even about one particular—money. Whatever their eccentricities as artistes, however much the norms of society didn't apply to them, they were all eyes and ears regarding this basic necessity. In this respect they were just like the rest of us.

The greatest of interval stretchers was Sandy Brown. I liked and admired Sandy very much but he was one of nature's great egotists and could be most infuriating.

With glass in hand and in full conversational flow (he was never anything else) no amount of chivvying would get him back to the stand. He would affect not to hear one's politely phrased first request and only heated badgering would beget some faint response, usually one of annoyance that his interminable discourse had been interrupted.

Before he returned to the bandstand, he would order another drink and commence another lengthy anecdote. Once he disappeared for more than his usual length of time, even. When he eventually showed, he said, " I bet you thought I was never coming back, eh?"

In situations like these the club promoter is completely nonplussed. It was never good politics to make a scene. One just had to bear with it.

When I did complain once about his unduly protracted break, his reply was that it was difficult to get served in the bar and in his opinion the interval should commence from the time he got served. I had no answer to match the ingenuity of that comeback.

I made a trip with a band to a club that was part of the 'milk round', a circuit of venues in the London area running on mid-week dates. They didn't pay much, but helped to buttress the weekly income. The pianist was driving and looked at his watch. " This is no good," he mumbled. " We'll be there on time at this rate." To delay the unthinkable he drove around several blocks, stopped to fill up with petrol and made another stop to buy cigarettes. After ten minutes of this deferment of arrival he said, " Better get to the hall, I suppose. Old Ken should be shitting himself by now."

When we entered the hall the promoter looked more relieved than annoyed. An American guest star was on the bill and, up to that moment he had a good crowd, a distinguished soloist but no band. Not that the audience were to be immediately entertained. The band wanted a drink and bowels and bladders had to be relieved. The drummer had to set up his kit. This took time. He was a conscientious performer, and everything had to be fixed just right.

After some testy chivvying from the promoter—fortunately the troubadours were in a fairly amenable mood—he and the audience heard the first note struck some twenty minutes after the band's arrival. The promoter was over one hurdle. His next problem would be to curtail the length of the interval. I was glad the problem was his and not mine, sympathetic though I was.

A film, *Living Jazz*, produced by Alan Lovell and Paddy Whannel, of the British Film Institute, and directed by Jack Gold, featured Bruce Turner's Band and several scenes were shot at the 'Six Bells'.

I was supposed to have a few lines of dialogue but a backer insisted that if this was to be the case, he too wanted to be in a scene at his club. My one and only chance of speaking on the silver screen was snatched away from me. I did appear for a second or two, silently addressing drummer John Armatage. Far from either of us being launched into a glittering screen career as a result of this telling scene, we now see each other every day, reporting back to the London Electricity Board's depot at Lithos Road, N.W.3 after reading meters for the Board.

Humphrey Lyttelton liked playing at the 'Six Bells' and one of the last sessions there was, happily and appropriately, a broadcast on B.B.C. Jazz Club celebrating Humph's twenty years as a bandleader.

It was heart-warming to see all the old faces on the bandstand. There was Keith Christie, Wally Fawkes, pianist Johnny Parker and, on a visit, Graeme Bell, as breezy and patronizing as ever.

A night for nostalgia and I hope the B.B.C. have retained the tape. It's a slice of British jazz history encapsulated into one evening's performance and commemorating the achievements and ability of Britain's leading jazzman.

Humph made a gracious and witty speech telling, quite inaccurately, how I first approached him at Friern Barnet to play with the Webb Band, how pleased he was to be celebrating his twentieth anniversary as a bandleader at a club in which I was the promoter, adding that if he asked me to come up and say a few words I would run a mile. He was right about this, but wrong about our first meeting. The evening's programme comprised of a warming-up session, followed by a taped broadcast. I had to muster the musicians from the bar for the prior session and started this harangue twenty minutes before the start of the session. The following scene was as traditional and recognizable in character as a Punch and Judy show with every facial response, line of dialogue and bodily movement totally predictable. It took all of fifteen minutes for the message to barely scratch the surface of their consciousness, and another five minutes before a reluctant move was made, and with hardly an acknowledgement of the individual urging them to return to the club room. In fact they barely seemed aware of my presence. When jazz musicians are in full verbal flight, entrepreneurs are neither seen nor heard. When the deadline approached, I became increasingly peremptory. I had a strong precedent on which to base my handling of the matter. I knew with whom I should be firm, who should be treated otherwise.

"Right!" I cried. "Off we go! *Parker! Christie! Green! Taylor! Lyttelton!* Ready, Wal?"

The 'Six Bells' Jazz Club started in March 1959. It lasted for ten years surviving, though only just, the rock and roll explosion of the early 'sixties that closed so many other jazz clubs. It might have been running as a jazz club now, but the owner-brewers thought the pub's situation in the King's Road, in swinging Chelsea, was the place for a new-style discotheque drinking house—it could hardly be described as a pub, not within my definition of the term.

The interior is completely transformed and there is a resident, all-smiling, all-gagging disc jockey with a transatlantic accent ploughing through a pile of pop records while stroboscopic lights fall on couples 'dancing' in the strangely asexual manner of our time.

There's none of the energetic jitterbugging, the music of the country's finest jazz musicians which I used to encourage in the good old days when one held one's partner.

"Ring Out Jazz" was the title of the club's obituary notice in the *Sunday Telegraph* written by Peter Clayton when the club closed in 1969.

As an agent I was continually dealing with club promoters, some of them quite memorable. There was a beery individual, well meaning, but not famed for his tact, who ran a club in the North. He mainly booked trad bands but, to give him credit, engaged mainstream bands out of a conviction that he should, but he was not prepared to leave it at that.

When Bruce Turner's Band appeared for him he lengthily addressed his members as the band stood waiting to commence playing. " Now lads, I know a lot of you are not going to like Bruce's Band. Like me, I know you prefer trad, but even if you don't like mainstream you should give them a fair hearing. Just give 'em a chance to show what they can do, aye, lads." This homily continued for some time whilst the band, already condemned out of the mouth of their employer, shifted uneasily behind him.

Some promoters had extraordinary excuses for poor business. " It's Lent ", or " It's before/after Christmas " or weather conditions be it ice, snow, fog, or sunshine. In fact if an attraction is strong enough it will draw crowds at any time of the year whatever the climatic conditions, or the competition.

The most unlikely, and hilarious, excuse I ever heard came from a promoter running a small club in a dingy hall in Putney, south-west London. One night business was particularly bad. " Of course," he said, surveying his meagre crowd, " it's the polo at 'Urlingham that does it. Once the season starts you've 'ad it." His premises were indeed near the highly exclusive Hurlingham Polo Club—a bastion of the rich where the sport of consorts and counts is played on a piece of turf probably worth several million pounds at current land values and the game played on this hallowed pasture was the rival to solid British trad being pounded out at a church hall every Thursday night.

There was a kindly couple who ran a very successful club in North London. They were generosity itself—and very good club promoters—but had strong racialist beliefs summed up in the following dialogue when someone asked them about their policy.

The man said, " It's New Orleans here, but we don't have any niggers. Isn't that right, Daisie?"

" Quite right, Ned. New Orleans, but no niggers."

At the time of writing, 1975, there are still a number of jazz clubs in the country, but mostly in pubs with free admission. It is but a fraction of the number flourishing in the trad boom and

group managed by Jim; a girl from Grimsby, Ann Moss, a charming and most efficient secretary; and Don Kingswell.

Don Kingswell was another of those rare birds that seem drawn, as if by some migratory instinct, to the entertainment business. He had been around for some time, notably as Cy Laurie's manager. I first got to really know him in 1962 when he was working for another agent. He was then in his early forties, plump, broad-shouldered, round-faced with hooded eyes, spoke with a slightly cockney accent and smoked incessantly. His salty observations had us all convulsed with laughter, although Ann affected to be horrified by his comments on sex and marriage. " Ooooooo, you are naughty!" she would say, in her soft Lincolnshire accent.

Don was also unconsciously funny, an odd contradiction as most funny people have an acute awareness of their own failings giving them a sharper appreciation of human lunacies generally. Don was totally unaware that he had any faults but with John, Ann and myself in constant proximity he was frequently informed of these. Congenitally incapable of owning up, it was information that he consistently rebutted.

His unconscious humour sprang from an extraordinarily limited vision of existence. To Don it was the immediacy of things that mattered. He didn't relate the parts of life, had no historical or social perspective, often used to say the first thing that came into his head, sometimes tactlessly, and frequently mispronounced.

I frequently mispronounce. For years my specialities were ' halycon ' for ' halcyon ' and ' public ' for ' pubic ' hair. Mick Mulligan and Jim Bray were unstinting in their corrections. With Don, the mispronunciations were a daily occurrence. Not that he would accept the corrections any more than he would take other criticisms. Like a plump seal caught in a net, he would wriggle furiously and employ the most ingenious terminology to prove he was right getting increasingly involved and contradictory as he struggled. It would have been so much simpler for him to own up, but that would have been contrary to one of his cardinal principles. It was in a spirit of banter for which we were known that I would jump on his mispronunciations.

" The word, Don, is specific, not pacific."

" *Oh*? You *sure*?"

" *Quite* sure."

" *I* don't think so."

" Will the Oxford Dictionary be acceptable to you as a reasonable arbiter?"

He would sense defeat. " If you say so, then ", a grudging acceptance, but only momentarily. He was always determined to have the last word, an infuriating characteristic. I attributed this to him being an only child and, typically, spoilt.

" True, I was spoilt, but I was worth spoiling. I was the apple *in* my mother's eye."

Some weeks later he returned to the argument. " I was listening to the news this morning and the announcer definitely said ' pacific ' and you'll grant that a B.B.C. announcer knows something about the Queen's English."

" He certainly does but he was probably referring to an ocean of that name, or even someone of that nature, and it's more than likely that you heard what you wanted to hear, very much a characteristic of yours."

" *Oh*, no! He definitely said it was a pacific case—what was it?—I know—a pacific case of foot and mouth disease."

" Want a bet on it?"

" *Oh*, no! You're always lucky!"

If Don and I had a bet and I won (and then only by offering the most overwhelming evidence) I was ' lucky ', never right.

Don was indeed plump (" Not for my size I'm not ") and vain (" Reckoned handsome—ask anyone "). I was in a pub with him and an old film starring a matinée idol of the 'thirties, Ray Milland, was on the television.

" Bloody hell," said Don. " He *does* look like me." Some, comparing Mr Milland's fame with Mr Kingswell's, might have put this observation the other way round, even were it true. Not Don. He didn't believe in hiding his light under a bushel. He repeatedly asserted, " People like me are hard to come by," a sentiment with which I was in total accord, although not necessarily for the reasons he gave.

At one stage in my see-saw career as an agent, I was working from my flat and if there was any summer sun streaming through the window I would take off my shirt. One hot day Don pounced. "A lot of spots on your back for someone who is supposed to be on a health food diet."

"True," I replied. "A bit of acne. Haven't had enough sun and air on my skin."

"That's not acne. They're bloody spots. My skin doesn't get any sun and air, but it's like velvet."

Don thought my vegetarianism, never really very strict, highly amusing. It provoked him to loud and prolonged guffaws. He claimed that all vegans looked ill and cited Bruce Turner, Cy Laurie, Tony Coe, Owen Bryce and myself. "Must be something in that funny diet of yours that draws the blood from the skin" was his considered opinion, seemingly unaware that his own complexion had the light brown sheen known as the night-club tan and well suited to his dark hair, slaked down with copious amounts of dressing in the manner of the pre-war dance band musicians.

He tackled me about organically grown foods, automatically suspicious and hostile about anything beyond his own horizons. I told him they were grown without the aid of artificial fertilizers, and chemical sprays.

"What fertilizers are used, then?" he asked, peering suspiciously over the rims of his spectacles. ("Nothing wrong with my eyesight. Can't read small print, that's all.")

"Compost heaps of rotting vegetables, or horse manure. Anything of vegetable origin."

"What about horses that eat meat, then? What about their shit, aye? Is that used?"

"Horses don't eat meat."

"What, none of them?"

"It would be a freak horse that does. They're natural vegetarians."

"You sure?"

"Quite sure."

"*Oh*, well, it's a lot of bollocks anyway!" As often happened with Don, the association of ideas would prompt one of his little gems. "I'm quite happy with my stable diet, thank you. You won't find anyone healthier than me." He was coughing over a cigarette as he spoke.

Natural history wasn't Don's strong point. He was a completely urban person. If he never saw another blade of grass, another tree or a bird in the sky, it wouldn't trouble him. To him, water was something that came out of a tap.

I confessed to flogging the diet issue, mainly to enjoy his responses.

" O.K. I'm filled with ' arbo-carbodrates ' and I drink—what do you call it—Teutonic [tannic] acid when I have a cup of tea, but I *enjoy* a cup of tea." He would heavily emphasize the word " enjoy " and mentioning certain foodstuffs he all but drooled. When he spoke of " fish " and " cream ", he would virtually quiver as the words left his mouth, and if eating something that made a strong assault on his taste buds, would emit an orgiastic " Aaaaaaaaaaaah !"

He wasn't to be persuaded that health reform principles were of any value. " All right, I'm full of toxins, but you rarely see me in a bad temper and doing moodies. I can't see your diet improves your temper, but then you drink too much."

Don was very censorious about the effects of alcohol, but was hardly ever without a cigarette in his mouth. This was a constant bone of contention (" discontention " as he put it) between us. " Most *normal* people smoke " was his counter argument to my bitter, ceaseless complaints that I, a non-smoker, was being slowly poisoned by his cigarette fumes. " It would be a good thing if a neuratic like you had a smoke. It would calm your nerves." " Neuratic " was one of his favourite portmanteau words, derived from neurotic and erratic. I find it difficult to use either of these proper words now that I have this rich and expressive hybrid at my disposal.

He would profess concern about my hypertension. " I know what would suit you," he said one morning. " A spell at a Kaput [he meant a Kibbutz]. But that probably wouldn't please you either. Too many arbo-carbodrates in the food, I expect. *Difficult* fellow. *Most* difficult," and he would shake his head as if I was quite beyond normal comprehension.

Don's firmly expressed idea of " relaxation " was to get home

The author and 'Red' Allen

The author, Bill Coleman, Lily Coleman and Doug Dobell

Bruce Turner's Jump Band at the 'Six Bells'. *Left to right:* Jim Bray, John Armatage, John Mumford, Bruce Turner, Collin Bates and John Chilton *(Photo: Russ Allen)*

Humphrey Lyttelton broadcasting from the 'Six Bells' to celebrate his twentieth year as a bandleader. *Left to right:* Tony Taylor (drums), Dave Green (bass), Humphrey Lyttelton, Wally Fawkes and Keith Christie *(Photo: John Hammond)*

as soon as possible (" No hanging around filthy pubs," he'd say, meaningfully) and change into his pyjamas, slippers and dressing-gown and watch T.V. without pause, food being served and consumed during his intense gaze; cigarettes, lighter, *T.V.* and *Radio Times* handily placed. Over the week-ends his viewing would total some twenty-four hours.

" That's the *sensible* way to behave," he would proclaim. " You won't catch me tearing around a cricket field when I should be *relaxing*. You should do the same. All that tearing about at your age can't do you any good. It wouldn't be so bad if you scored any runs. You give yourself a lot of aggro for nothing. *Relax*! Take things easy like I do."

He mocked my cricketing, well aware that my enthusiasm was considerably in excess of my ability. When I was working from my flat I used to keep a bat handy and essay a few strokes during the lunch break, accompanied by the cry " WHAM!" when I fancied the ball had made full contact with the meat of the bat. Don would launch into an imaginary conversation with a client.

" Ah come in, Mr Bradley. Do sit down. Nice to see you again. Have a cigarette, Mr Bradley. Sorry about the broken glass. Mr Godbolt was having a few whams. The ball was a bit uppish, he was going to hook it for four when he made contact with the light bulb. He won't be long, Mr Bradley. Just popped over to the pub for a livener. He likes a drink, Mr Bradley. Keen cricketer, though, not that he scores any runs. Pity, things might be a bit cosier on a Monday morning if he did."

" No, Mr Bradley, I don't play myself. Not on your life. I *relax* on Sundays. Too old to be charging round a cricket field. So is he, Mr Bradley, but he won't own up. Do you play, Mr Bradley? No? I expect you're like me. Like to get your feet up over the week-end. You've got to *relax* Mr Bradley, haven't you?"

Don had no hesitation in telling me what others thought about me. Invariably the comments were critical. It appeared from these readily imparted reports that not a single person had a good word to say for me.

" I went to the Chinese Fish Shop in Berwick Street for lunch. Wouldn't suit *you*, of course. Too much clatter. Too many

K

arbo-carbodrates. I got a good whack of stodge down me. Large piece of cod, double portion of chips, a gherkin and white bread and butter. Finished off with a nice cup of Teutonic acid. It was *lovely*! Real food. Not like your cranky nutmeat cutlets. Saw John Cox there. He asked me if I was still with you and I told him. 'Bloody Hell,' he said, 'Don't know how you stand it '."

Only once did he impart a favourable opinion, but he hedged on this, even. "You can't tell with him, though. He's such a two-faced bastard."

Don had a wide command of verbal images. "Shooting Gallery" for lavatories (where people "urianated"). "The Enemy" for Mrs Kingswell, "Nannygoat Shitting on Tin" for a vocalist who didn't meet with his approval, "Come Before The Milkman" for premature ejaculation, "Nonsense" for the penis, and "Knocking a Round off" for the male contribution to coitus.

There were many others. "Haven't got a pot to piss in" to describe his impecunity, "A short session of death" for an afternoon nap, "The Downstairs Department" for the genitals and when pontificating about moderation in all things he would proclaim "There's a difference between shitting and tearing your arse."

And, daily, the picturesque mispronunciations. "Yes, thank you, I'm in fine fetter", "Aniahalation of affection", "They charged exuberant prices", "I'll reincarnate that enquiry for you, Mr Bradley" and "Look here, son, I want a complicit answer from you" and "phantasglorium" for phantasmagoria were gems that helped to pass the day enjoyably.

Sometimes it was the cart before the horse. "Envy with green" and "They were packed-jam together" were two lovely examples and when promising to put up offers to groups' managements, he referred to them as "powers to be". These mispronunciations were richly comic. It's when words are deliberately mispronounced for humorous effect that the intention is never fulfilled and never as graphically descriptive as unconscious slips and unknowing mispronunciation, at which Don was the Guv'nor.

Don was the supreme Philistine. He was quite convinced that

people only *pretended* to enjoy classical music. No one ever really *read* the *Sunday Times* or the *Observer* or their daily counterparts. He stoutly affirmed that they were merely for show and that they acted as covers for concealing the lurid Sundays which *he* read. He had a few searing comments to make about *avant-garde* modes, be it music, painting or sculpture.

He was a convinced monarchist and extremely right-wing in his politics. If John or myself expressed anti-monarchist or left-wing views, he had a familiar automatic response. " You people," (his favourite phrase for those whose opinions were not in accord with his own) " should go and live in Russia." He strongly disapproved of public entertainers expressing political opinions, although only if they were left-wing sentiments.

His behaviour, he would have us believe, was *the* criterion. One morning I put some memos on his desk before he arrived. As I heard him puffing up the stairs, I motioned to Ann to remain silent and I hid behind the door.

He picked up the notes. " What's all this? More silly bits of paper? Huh! Bloody nonsense! What does he think he's doing? Must be off his head! This is no good! Pity I'm not running this business." After he had maligned me further, I suddenly appeared from behind the door. His jowls dropped and he accused me of deceptive behaviour. Came the classic criterion, often repeated. " *I* don't do things like that!"

Don joined me in 1963. In our early days together he had a strange compulsion to take an automatically opposite point of view to mine and if I suggested that an agency be approached to take a certain band or group he would instantly rebut the idea claiming that the party I had suggested wouldn't be the least interested.

After pressure, he would reluctantly pick up the phone, snorting impatiently at something so patently useless. Once he reached the office concerned, his phraseology would indicate the answer he wanted to vindicate his own view.

" Hello, George. Don't suppose you're interested in X group? No? Thought so. Not in your line, is it? Sorry to have troubled you." He would replace the phone and triumphantly look up at me with an apposite comment. I would explode in fury, he would retaliate and Ann would flee the office in fright. Later we were in accord, but not without periodic shout-ups.

It was his vanity that lay behind his rejection of my ideas. He couldn't bear to be in the wrong, and this vanity knew no bounds. In one of our heated exchanges, he resorted to quoting a girl who allegedly had told him she thought I was his father, so youthful did he look alongside a haggard old man like me. I'm a few years younger than Don and even allowing that the ravages of time and worry have left their mark, it was really stretching things for him to eagerly accept the observation as being true, but that was Don.

He was a consummate actor who could wring pathos out of any situation to gain sympathy. If hurt, he would lean his head on one side, like a mystified dog unsure why his master was scolding him, a pose calculated to moisten every eye in the house.

I was extremely fond of Don. The vanity, boastfulness and reluctance to admit faults were combined with a considerable charm, a generosity of spirit and a memorable wit. I've seen him keep a roomful of people convulsed with laughter for an entire evening. He could unaffectedly treat with kings and commoners alike, was very conscientious in his job, excelling at tour management, the best in the business.

Getting the show on the road and seeing it run as smoothly as possible was a matter of professional pride with him and he has since gone to America to manage one of their top groups— Sha-Na-Na. Dressed in striped formal wear and doffing a bowler hat, he introduces them in a mock Hooray accent. It's a spectacle I'd love to behold.

Don was a good friend. A good man to have at one's side. Our improbable relationship lasted for seven years and he came into my business at a time when the entire shape and colour of the business generally was about to be drastically transformed.

BOMBSHELL HITS THE
PROFESSION

During the 'fifties the popular music scene was extremely varied
with big dance bands, trad and modern jazz bands, solo singers
like Dickie Valentine, Frankie Vaughan, Alma Cogan and—
let us not forget—Eddie 'Golden Trumpet' Calvert. Newly
emerging were the rock and roll stars—Tommy Steele, Vince
Eager, Duffy Power and Cliff Richard. These were a portent
of things to come.

On I.T.V. there was a show called " Hoots Mon " featuring
Lord Rockingham's Eleven, a unit of highly competent dance
band musicians cynically, lucratively, playing rock and roll.

Humphrey Lyttelton wrote of rock and roll : " The rhythmic
essence of jazz, extracted, simplified, exaggerated . . . a formula
of the heavy off-beat on the drums and honking saxophones . . .
suggestive lyrics . . .". He lashed into " Hoots Mon ". The
show's producer, Jack Good, retaliated by averring that the
musicians concerned were better than Humph. Humph replied,
" I've no doubt these musicians can read music better than I
can. No-one denies the pro her technique . . ."

Steve Race wrote in the *Melody Maker*, " Viewed as a social
phenomenon the current craze for rock and roll is one of the
most terrifying things ever to have happened in popular music.
And, of course, we follow the lead of the American music
industry. When Father turns, we all turn."

Many believed rock and roll to be a passing phase. Agent
Harold Davison, quoted in the *Melody Maker*, said, " My bands
will be featuring it whilst the demand lasts, like they featured
Be-pop and the mamba. But any band that ties its destiny to
rock and roll is likely to die when the craze burns out."

The rock and roll craze of the 'fifties was but a mere tremor presaging the explosion to come. It was not until 1962 that the volcano erupted with a cataclysmic fury when the *Melody Maker* could have used their favourite war-time heading " Bombshell Hits The Profession " with every justification. Two British groups, the Beatles and the Rolling Stones, were the catalysts of the upheaval.

Not one of the previous developments in popular music this century—Edwardian ballads, 'twenties dance and jazz music, 'thirties swing, 'forties Be-bop and revivalism—had anything like the shattering impact made by these two groups dramatically rising from obscurity in the early 'sixties. This transformation of the popular music scene was sociologically highly significant. It was largely created by the newly affluent teenager buying vast numbers of records by performers whose music and life-style was in accord with their own youthful thinking and aspirations. The teenagers' choice of idols affected a mass audience. There could hardly have been a soul in the land who didn't know the name and face of every Beatle and Mick Jagger of the Rolling Stones. This couldn't be said of any other combination of singers and instrumentalists in any other area of popular music at any time. This revolution wasn't engineered by businessmen. In fact many entrepreneurs in all parts of the business had initially rejected those artists so much a part of the change, but soon the record industry was athrob with frantic activity. Thousands of records were made in an attempt to cash in on the Rock n' Roll bonanza. A mass of hitherto unknown young faces became news, the Beatles were to become millionaires, or should have been, and the ' professional ' musician turned rock and roller faded from sight. Jazz reeled from the blast; the touring large dance band all but disappeared; there was much less emphasis on the solo singer; Eddie Calvert emigrated to South Africa.

These shattering changes were to alter the pattern of many agents' activities, me included. Jazz clubs, and the bands who relied on them for the best part of their income folded. At the height of the trad boom there were forty bands on the road. The number quickly dwindled to a mere half dozen. Understandably, rock and roll groups proliferated. If two groups of working-class boys could achieve fame and fortune with voice and guitar, the example was there for thousands to follow.

From the mid 'fifties I had been booking jazz bands into the Mardi Gras, Liverpool, owned by Jim Ireland, who managed the Swinging Blue Jeans, whom I represented. They had a minor chart success with a song called " Too Late Now ", and followed up with a smash hit, " Hippy Hippy Shake ". It raced to No. 2 in the Hit Parade charts of most papers and to No. 1 in one publication.

I take no credit for the Blue Jeans' record success but some praise, perhaps, for the manner in which my office handled the situation. We did the job in which we were experienced and the mechanics of booking are the same for a Hit Parade group as for one utterly unknown. The financial outcome of the former happens to be considerably more rewarding. That hit record changed everything. It was the same group, with the same act, the same material but with an important difference. They were in the Top Ten, the pop metamorphosis. Before " Too Late Now ", £30 an engagement was the norm; after " Too Late Now ", £75; after " Hippy Hippy Shake " between £250 and £300 a night.

With this increased income I wasn't unwilling to adapt to the new scene. It was no longer possible to live by jazz bands alone, and I wasn't the only jazz agent, getting on a bit, to be found sitting amongst screaming adolescents in concert halls wondering what it was all about. It was imperative we found out. Or go under.

Our daily contacts broadened. They were no longer just the friendly coterie of like-minded people that made up the business side of jazz. That familiar camaraderie remained, if somewhat shaken, but the daily round now included people previously unknown to us. I continued to book jazz bands where the demand continued and on Saturday nights I was amongst people I really knew at the ' Six Bells ', but our daily preoccupation was booking the emergent groups, particularly the Swinging Blue Jeans.

" Hippy Hippy Shake " temporarily changed my status as an agent. It was relatively short-lived glory that I found not only profitable but highly amusing and extremely illuminating.

Having been through the mill for so long, I can solemnly avow that I regarded this turn of events as a sweet bonus and I had no illusions that I could soon be returning to the struggle of *pursuing* business and, indeed, it wasn't that long before I was back to the familiar struggle of keeping office and staff together.

But it was fun whilst it lasted! Agents to whom I had never spoken before would ring and solicitously enquire after my health. Prior to this they hadn't been too concerned with my well-being, probably because they had never heard of me. Nor had I heard of them.

After receiving assurances that my health was sound and their delight in this knowing no bounds, I would be invited to lunch. This concern for my health and appetite was typical of the business ethic. Success, or associated success, was the yardstick by which the individual was measured.

Another agent then new to me rang. " Hello, Jim bhoy. Did you have a nice Christmas?" The enquiry surprised me a little, as the calendar read 7th February.

This new status had its moments when dealing with certain hard-headed promoters. One of them was eager to place the Blue Jeans in an extended concert tour. I went to see him with more than bookings for the Blue Jeans in my sights. I had another group of Jim Ireland's that badly needed exposure and a nation-wide tour with big names was just the opportunity. I made it an implicit condition that one wouldn't be booked without the other. I didn't have to make the stipulation in so many words. My meaning was perfectly clear. " This is blackmail," spluttered the promoter, a ruthless operator who wouldn't have hesitated a second to apply the same methods if it suited him. I walked out of that office with a bit of a power complex, just for once.

Robert Stigwood, currently a highly successful West End theatre impresario, then promoting pop concerts, wanted to speak to me about booking the Blue Jeans. He was apologetic about being unable to come and see me owing to pressure of business but if he sent a car around to pick me up, would I be prepared to come along and discuss a deal?

An enormous shiny limousine, driven by a uniformed chauffeur, appeared outside my office in Wardour Street to collect me. As I stepped into this elegant motor, I casually looked around to see if any of my contemporaries were about. They would have had no trouble in seeing me. Ostentatiously, I sat in full view, there and back. The negotiation was plain sailing. The Blue Jeans were in the Top Ten. I'd expended a lot more time and nervous energy trying to get a fifty-pound engagement for Mick Mulligan before that.

About four years later I was in Stigwood's office haggling with one of his minions about an inter-office commission dispute when the impresario walked in, looked straight through me and walked out without a word. I was lucky to get any commission out of this haggle and I caught the 73 bus back to my office.

The Swinging Blue Jeans were a good, musicianly group with a highly professional approach to their work but, initially, the success of " Hippy Hippy Shake " went to their heads a little. Like so many other young men they were unable fully to adjust to sudden success. Ray Ennis, the leader, was given to bawling me out on patent trivialities, and one of the group, who left it shortly afterwards, felt his position to be so exalted he would imperiously summon the road manager into his presence and make peremptory commands.

" Bert! Hand me my guitar!"

The instrument was literally under his nose, but he saw himself as a big star and the road manager a minion to obey as commanded.

As it happened this particular road manager basked in reflected glory and by his arrogant and high-handed attitude to people in the business generally, it was obvious that he flicked some of the stardust on to himself.

Later, when economic truths faced the group, we all became the best of friends and I remained their agent for seven years, without a contract, right up to the time I left the business.

We quickly discovered that a group's fees for their public appearances were strictly related to their chart successes, irrespective of any intrinsic value. Much depended on good material, and only a small proportion of the mass of material offered was suitable. Few had hit potential, but publishers were a pushing species. During the success of " Hippy Hippy Shake " my phone was hot with calls from them. Speaking from the bottom of their hearts they would fervently assure me they had " The very number for the bhoys, bhoy. Must be No. 1, bhoy."

The search for material was unceasing, the group, and agent, benefiting considerably when a record made the charts, the latter struggling to maintain prices when the records flopped, even after receiving a large number of plugs on radio and TV.

Week after week new groups emerged to take the place of those who had fallen by the wayside not having had a hit record for six months, that period, from an agent's point of view, being the maximum duration that he could hold prices.

The contemptuous term ' One-Hit Wonders ' entered pop terminology. One hit wasn't enough to sustain prices, but most groups and their managers wouldn't acknowledge any drop in drawing power and insisted that peak figures were maintained, turning down work at lesser fees rather than make the adjustment. The agent was equally reluctant to see a reduction that meant less commission, but he was in the best position to assess the market value of his groups and could only advise on these truths, not that they were always acceptable, especially to those whose ascent to fame had been sudden.

When a new record came out the agent joyfully spread the glad tidings. " They've got a new single coming out next month. It's really something else. *Must* make the charts. The record company are going to give it the treatment. They think it's a winner." I intoned that litany a thousand times in my daily conversations with other agents over the years and I reached the stage where I was mocking myself for boring repetition of a worthless boast. Moreover, it may not have been true that the record company were going to give the record any more than nominal advertising, especially if sales for their previous release had been low. Significantly, I didn't hear from the publishers who had previously been hot on the phone. Naturally, they wanted to place their material with the currently successful groups.

These were just a few of the variables that we came to recognize in this strange ephemeral world of pop music. At times it was quite dream-like, a phantasmagoria of constant fluctuation but, firmly rooted in reality, were the sharply rising overheads. The landlord and telephone service, alone, were not concerned with the varying fortunes of pop groups. Despite the increased gross income it was a commercial quicksand we were treading.

I got to know the doyen of all pluggers, the late Sidney Green of Chappell's Publishing Company. He was plugging one of the Blue Jeans best records, " You're No Good ", when I first met him. Sid (" Sid the Yid " he called himself) was a most delightful man, totally preoccupied with his calling. Although well into his fifties he adapted himself to the rock boom with a professional thoroughness. He bombarded groups, managers and agents, with material, and haunted Radio and TV producers with records.

He would brook no arguments from these young men. It was he, with his vast experience of the business, who was doing them a favour by letting them have records that would enhance the popularity of their programmes, and their reputations with their superiors.

But he had his problems. If a tune of his was recorded by two or more artistes, it was rare that more than one would make the charts.

" You think you've got trubbles, bhoy," said Sid in a thick Jewish accent, his hand splayed out Jewish fashion as he spoke. " Here I am with a hit with ' Hello Dolly ' by Kenny Ball and Frankie Vaughan's telling me I'm not trying hard enough with his version. My life! Can I help it if Kenny's version does better?" Sid realized this might be construed as criticism of Vaughan and quickly added a rider, " *Luvly* bhoy, Frankie. A great singer." At that moment it was unlikely that Frankie was reciprocal in his sentiments about Sid as a plugger.

There was litigation in America over " Hello Dolly ", a composer alleging plagiarism. " That's the trubble with hits, bhoy," said Green. " Get yourself one and you get yourself a lawsuit " and in this instance, into Mr Vaughan's black books.

The Blue Jeans didn't repeat their " Hippy Shake " success but occasionally appeared in the charts over two or three years. Their last hit was a version of a tune called " Don't Make Me Over ". I sent the record to the producer of the TV show " Sunday Night At The London Palladium ", fully aware that it could easily be overlooked amongst dozens of other recordings and made the usual follow-up calls. The producer had mislaid the record, but his secretary had praised it. He asked for another copy on the strength of her recommendation. On such apparently slender threads are reputations enhanced! I virtually sprinted round to his office with the record and the Blue Jeans got a booking on the show.

The day of the performance was of great moment to Don. To him the Palladium was holy ground. To tread those hallowed boards meant you had truly arrived.

He had enjoyed an association with the theatre in his affluent days (before, as he often implied, he was reduced to working for someone like me) when he would hire a box every Sunday afternoon for the Ted Heath Swing Sessions, load it with drinks and cigarettes and act as host for the cast of the show. Don always referred lovingly to " The Green ", an abbreviation of " Greengage ", rhyming slang for stage, and his association with show-biz went back to the late 'thirties when he used to escort Vera Walsh, later known as Vera Lynn, to her first professional engagement with Charlie Kunz's Band at the Club Casani, off Regent Street, in the late 'thirties.

On the day, he shook hands with all the musicians in Jack Parnell's resident orchestra, puffed with pride that ' his ' boys were appearing on this show of shows. It was an atmosphere that made an unfavourable impression on me. I have never been prey to show-biz mystique. It always struck me as the gold that never really glistered, and I hated all that spurious and vomitory hand-shaking and back-slapping that is a mandatory exercise amongst its forever beaming performers. Don found my attitude utterly incomprehensible.

Not that I was unhappy about the Blue Jeans at this shrine of admass entertainment and had there been any bowing or scraping to be done before the producer and his staff I would have genuflected without a moment's hesitation, an agent's pride, if any, being entirely expendable.

It was a boost for the Blue Jeans (and their agent) who had been out of the limelight for some time, and they performed extremely well, Ray Ennis, particularly. After they had finished their spot, I made for the nearest pub with a happy but exhausted Don. He had been at the theatre since ten that morning.

There were a few wives and girlfriends of the group in the pub and I hesitantly introduced myself to one of the girlfriends not quite certain who she was. She introduced her mother and father, and mum, misunderstanding what I had said about me being unsure who they were, looked at her extremely attractive daughter and replied, " Oh, yes, we're often mistaken for each other."

At that moment Don joined the company and was completely thrown by a claim that can only be described as exaggerated. His jaw dropped as he took an involuntary, comparing glance. As it happened it was the sort of flattering comparison he would have made, had he thought of it. Don could lay the smooch-treacle on with a trowel if he reckoned it would enhance his image or further his ends in any way. I had to look away from the flummoxed Kingswell in case I erupted with laughter. Mum also knew a lot about the business. Looking intently at me she expressed the opinion that the group should be doing much better than they were.

At the time there were searing allegations that charts were being rigged by unscrupulous agents, managers and record producers and the *Melody Maker* rightly came out heavily against this skulduggery and changed its method of compiling retailers' returns. It was undoubtedly a sincere attempt to stop any machinations that could affect its long-standing reputation, but the business was too diversified and involved too many people on a nationwide scale for there to be a completely effective prevention of these abuses.

I confess I would have had no compunction in trying to fiddle a chart entry—had I known how—rationalizing that if records were being engineered into the charts this would reduce genuine chances of my groups' records making an entry—not that I convinced myself, even, of this argument's validity.

The chart-riggers were not the only sharp wheelers and

dealers in the business. The beat boom attracted many shady individuals, as blood attracts sharks and, as with their marine counterparts, these appeared to come from nowhere.

There were apparently easy pickings to be had from this vast sea of activity. If one of these predators could, say, book a hall with a thousand capacity and charge, say, fifteen shillings (now 75p) admission his gross return on a capacity house would be £750.

If a promoter paid a top group £300 and hire of the hall, advertising, staff and support group came to £100 he stood, at best, to make a profit of £350, not bad for a night's work. But he may have miscalculated. If the group had dropped in popularity since he first booked them, or the area had been packed with similar attractions, just before or after his event—or the pop equivalent of " Polo at 'Urlingham " perhaps—he could have a poor attendance. Without the funds to cover costs he could disappear into the night and never be seen again. There were many of these fly-by-nights.

When these incidents became commonplace, payment in advance became the rule when we didn't know the promoter. It didn't necessarily follow that payment was assured when we did. Nor was it always the promoter at fault. He could be anxiously waiting at the entrance of a hall packed with impatient customers and no sign of the group. Sometimes they didn't show up at all. Money came so easily to some of the young stars that if there was a more pleasurable alternative to a booking it was the engagement that went by the board. They were shortsighted enough to think their earning power would last indefinitely. The situation got so bad that potential customers in a town wouldn't pay for admission until they had seen physical evidence of the group's arrival.

Another aspect of the new scene was the number of groups insistent that the agent should travel vast distances to hear them. Proud fathers would appear at the office holding demonstration records of their sons' talents, some with only filial affirmation of vocal and instrumental ability. " My boy's got a fine new group " was a phrase I heard a few times.

I listened to as many as possible. The dread fear that a segment of the Beatles' history might be repeated haunted us all.

Segment it may have been but still a tale of epic proportions considering the Beatles' staggering financial turnover.

Despite playing to riotous acclaim in Liverpool, no one in London—agents, promoters, recording and publishing companies—were interested. They were just another beat group from the provinces. When they achieved unprecedented global fame in an astonishingly short time, there was much hand-wringing and sleepless nights from those who had had the opportunity to earn fortunes from this bonanza but had been blind to their chances.

Don Kingswell was one of the first to be approached by Brian Epstein, the Beatles' manager. Don was road manager of a package that featured the American rock and roll star, Little Richard.

Before the tour commenced the organizer gave Don firm instructions that when the show played Liverpool, on no account was a group called the Beatles to play more than two numbers, further advising him that the promoter of the show also managed the Beatles and would insist on more, a delicate situation where Don was advised to " use his loaf ". Don used his loaf, the Beatles played only two numbers and a possible fortune slipped through his fingers. Epstein asked him to represent the group in London and Don replied, " Mr Epstein, there are five thousand groups like that in London all looking for work. They wouldn't stand a chance. You keep them working round here where they are known."

Later, when Don proclaimed that he " hadn't got a pot to piss in " he ruefully meditated on what might have been.

He wasn't the only one.

Most people in the jazz world congratulated me on my good fortune in representing a hit parade group, but there were exceptions. I was in a pub prior to attending a concert featuring the great U.S. negro trumpeter, Red Allen, when jazz record-shop owner Doug Dobell lurched up to me and venomously hissed, " *Godbolt! Traitor to Jazz!*"

On another occasion I walked into David Bilk's office and received a touch of the ideologicals from Frank Parr. He had been a fervent, if expatriate, Liverpudlian but bewailed he'd lost pride in his home-town since its new claim to fame was the spawning ground of ' Merseybeat '.

As he was handling Acker Bilk's date sheet, he could earn a living and retain his ideologicals, but was hardly in a position to adopt such a stern moral posture, as he and his office were actively concerned (as I pointedly remarked) in the promotion of All-In Wrestling, surely (as I pointedly remarked) the least edifying of spectacles with the possible exception of the Miss World contests.

David, not normally one to lose an opportunity to score a point, hastily put a clamp on any further observations about my fall from grace, probably because if the opportunity had arisen for his office to represent any of these emergent attractions he wouldn't have been too bothered about Frank's ideological objections.

Generously I forgave Frank for his strictures. Most jazzers, including myself, had long adopted moral postures about our beloved music, a habit ingrained after long membership of a minority group, and, indeed, I was strenuously protesting the value of jazz over the music that was now making me some real money—albeit temporarily.

In 1963 the *Melody Maker* carried a five-column spread entitled, " Dr Godbolt or—How I Learned To Stop Worrying and Love the Boom ". It comprised an interview with myself approached from the angle of a long-time jazz booker/enthusiast now representing a successful rock and roll group.

I answered the questions fairly objectively, but rationalized about the quality of rock and roll. The sentiments I expressed were more than a slight bending of my true beliefs, but professionally I could hardly do otherwise. A plum had fallen into my lap and it would have been ungracious, unbusinesslike and uneconomic to knock it. However, I insisted that jazz, after nigh on fifty years as a meaningful music, wouldn't die overnight.

Apart from Don's trenchant comments about certain aspects of the scene that gave us, and our visitors, unceasing amusement, comic relief poured through the letter-box—a host of unsolicited testimonials to human naïvety, stupidity and optimism.

In the latter regard I contributed my bit with a ceaseless flow of correspondence and publicity hand-outs to bookers, agents, promoters and producers. No doubt some of the claims I made on behalf of my artistes bordered on the fanciful. It was my business to sell and if I thought I could get away with a little exaggeration I would have no hesitation, but I hope that none of my correspondence was as bizarre, cheeky and comical as some we received.

One manager wrote: " We would like to know if you can offer any prospects for a group of our calibre. We have been on the Mersey scene for some considerable time but have not had much success due to our being with the wrong agent. Because of existing contracts I have been unable to write to you in the past, but would like to know if you are interested in a group much better than the Swinging Blue Jeans ".

Another, in a pathetically illiterate scrawl, wrote: " I red your address in the *Musical Express* and it gives me great pleasure to write and ask for an ordition. My name is ———— and I am a pop singer."

Another: " Dear Sirs, Is there any chance of joining your agency. I have not had any previous experience, but would like a singing career. My age is thirty-nine."

We received a glossy photograph of a beautiful coloured girl with protuberant breasts. The accompanying letter stated that " She does a half-hour spot and really knows how to use what she's got. Her fee is £100, but this is negotiable ". Details of what sort of performance she offered were not given.

Another hilarious letter: " Dear Madam (!), I have a girl of twenty years of age. She has a clear, strong voice, low range, has practised modern stage techniques with a professional guitarist. She is coloured, not black."

A letter from Cheshire: " Further to our enquiries regarding the Swinging Blue Jeans I'm sorry to say that the promoter has decided not to use this type of act but has now booked some musical clowns instead ".

A card from Ipswich gave us the following information:

L

From Way Out
for Beat Entertainment
HOWLING LAWRENCE
and his XXXXXXXXX
Arabians

" Arabians " was written in words under the almost inked-
out but clearly discernible " Phallic Symbols ". Presumably the
manager had got cold feet at the last minute and attempted to
obliterate the words that might have been regarded as offensive
in 1962.

Nowadays he wouldn't be too concerned with our prurient
susceptibilities in a scene which has one group called " Hard
Meat " who rubber stamp their contracts with an illustration of
an erect phallus, and another group with the name of " Brewer's
Droop " although, understandably they don't use any corres-
ponding illustrative stamp.

Quite intentionally hilarious was a Christmas card from a
pop group leader called Screaming Lord Sutch. He stood as
Independent candidate for Huyton, Lancs in the 1966 General
Election. His principal opponent was Harold Wilson and with
commendable cheek arranged for a photographer to be on hand
at the moment he, a good loser (he lost his deposit) proffered his
hand to the victorious Mr Wilson.

The Rt Hon. Harold Wilson looks at Lord Sutch with an
expression of grudging admiration, two police officers nearby
have expressions of horror and incredulity. It's a gem.

Inside the card was Sutch's message;
" Sutch congratulates the Top of the Land,
By a Shake of the Hand,
Governments Come and Governments Go
But Lord Sutch Stays There,
Friend or Foe ".

During this flow of correspondence my name was frequently
mis-spelt. Godding, Gitbolt, Goblin, G'odbolt, Bodgegott, Gobbo,
Goabit, Bodgolder and Godlio were a few of the variations and
there was one addressed to God Bolt Agency, but one young lady
got the name right.

She wrote : " Dear Mr Godbolt, You have a quite divine

Nordic sounding name but I'm afraid I won't be booking the bands you suggested, I've booked the Temperance Seven instead ".

A lady in Hampshire was an ardent fan of the Swinging Blue Jeans and repeatedly booked them for charity dances she organized. On the telephone one day she was insistent they were the group she wanted. No one else would do.

" You see," she gushed, " They're not just a pop group to me. I regard them as *human beings*!"

There were no further eruptions comparable to the emergence of the Beatles and the Rolling Stones but rock and roll and its derivatives continued to dominate the popular music scene.

The jazz bands who survived the bombshell continued to work steadily to appositely ageing audiences and some of the solo singers stayed in business, including the omnipresent Frankie Vaughan.

13

WHAT DO YOU ACTUALLY DO ALL DAY?

I was asked this question, in all seriousness, by a member of the Ravers Eleven. He obviously harboured the usual misconceptions about an agent's slothful, parasitical life. Tongue in cheek, I gave a fanciful description of a languorous existence, of riches casually acquired on the backs of creative artistes. He believed me. I could reasonably have asked *him* the same question. He was a stockbroker!

In truth an agent's life is generally hard graft, with a lot more pitfalls and setbacks than in most commerce, his office a smoky, crowded clearing house for the manifold aspects of the business.

In the few productive hours each day, he works under considerable pressure and his primary activity, booking engagements, is constantly impeded by a stream of callers: band and group leaders, their roadies, and members of the groups looking in ostensibly to enquire about engagements but with the ulterior motive of chatting up the secretary or slyly, sometimes blatantly, examining the date sheets to see how much work and at what money other groups are getting.

The trivia and minutiae of agency procedure devour the agent's time, time that should be spent on bookings. This necessity forever maggots away in his brain. Time forever haunts him as unfilled dates loom nearer, and he can do without unnecessary callers, especially young ladies with urgent reasons for getting in touch with musicians.

The agent booking 'one-night stands' thinks primarily of Thursdays, Fridays, Saturdays and Sundays, these being the days obviously favoured by the promoters and an agent can be less than popular with a group if they play the Thursday, Saturday and Sunday out of town necessitating a ' night out ' or a return to London with attendant expense in both cases.

Much depends on the popularity of the group. If it's one that's in demand the agent's problems are of a more desirable kind. He is rejecting rather than seeking offers.

Pushing the unknowns and the unwanteds is especially time-consuming, involving expense hardly commensurate with the commission gain, but agencies persist with these in the simple hope that they will build popularity or because someone has backed them financially and is breathing heavily down the agent/booker's neck. If the office is a management/agency unit, like the Bron Organization, it's likely that the individuals doing the heavy breathing are in close proximity.

This is the stage when new groups are eager for work. " Man, we need the exposure. Send us anywhere. We'll make it if we get out there and show 'em." However, if the public are eventually clamouring for them the agent's next problem is persuading them to accept the engagements offered. This is the stage when members of groups suffer a now fashionable pop scene ailment called ' nervous exhaustion ', often necessitating cancellation of engagements. I have known times when this unfortunate condition, seemingly a corollary of rising popularity and concomitant indulgence, appeared to reach epidemic proportions.

Can't engagement contracts be enforced? If agents, managers, promoters and artistes were to take legal action every time there was a contravention of contract they would be daily parading in and out of the courts, the lawyers would wax even fatter and the agent would never see his phone, much less use it. Unless a lot of money is involved, all parties tend to shrug off non-fulfilment and hope that future contracts will be implemented and, if so, the agent, traditionally, is the last to get paid and then usually only split commission (five per cent).

He is only the intermediary. The client/promoter is the actual employer and, understandably, outraged when a group fails to arrive. One wrote to the *Melody Maker* indignantly railing against agents and managers who failed to exercise proper control over their artistes. He failed to differentiate between agents and managers and used the old saw about both being ' parasites '. He was prey to the usual misconceptions about the respective functions of agents and managers.

Agents do not 'control' artistes, nor do they 'send' them to engagements. They submit offers to an artiste, or his manager, it being the latter's responsibility to see that contracts are fulfilled, granted that the very idea of exercising any control over some of the pustular delinquents in the pop world is a joke. A classroom of convicted hooligans in a reform school would be easier to handle.

The hazards and frustrations of booking in the pop world are considerable. There is a high non-fulfilment rate. In my experience jazz bands invariably made their engagements even if, on some occasions, their condition on arrival was quite deplorable. This sense of obligation cannot be said of many pop groups.

Nowadays an agent never counts his commission before he sees it. If he has, on a particular week-end, a specific number of exchanged contracts (both parties having the signature of the other) amounting to X pounds, this is no guarantee of payment. By the time the disaster roll is called on the Monday morning that figure could be X-minus. Not that he has to wait until Monday mornings to be appraised of non-fulfilment. Over the week-end reverse charge calls, usually between the dreaded hours of six and nine p.m. come as no surprise.

There are many variations on the haunting theme of non-fulfilment. A group, in possession of a signed contract, arrive and find no engagement to fulfil. The promoter may have fled, or double-booked. If the former situation the group and agent can only accept the bad luck, but if it's the latter there is a telephone call—reverse charge, of course—to the agent instructing him to sort the matter out. I swear those reverse-charge calls would ring in an ominously recognizable fashion. These defections are an everyday occurrence in a business peopled with unscrupulous promoters and young men with no sense of responsibility suddenly rising to fame.

After non-fulfilment the agent has to sort out the mess. He has lost his commission, but doesn't want to lose a client, or goodwill. If it's one of his own groups that has defected he has to put the best possible face on the situation, especially if he happens to know that the lead guitarist had had a heavy night at one of the West End clubs favoured by rock musicians and awoke, late in the day, with an iron turban bolted into his throbbing head and a host of serpents squirming in his stomach.

In this unfortunate, if self-inflicted, condition the prospect of a trip to Cleethorpes alarmed him to the point of terror. He may not have ever fancied a trip to Cleethorpes, but this nervous exhaustion put the final seal on his reluctance.

If the defecting group is represented by another agent, the agent or manager is likely to aggressively plead, " Can I help it if one of the lads had a heavy night at the Speakeasy? I'm not their bloody nursemaid!"

Assuming the group arrives and plays, they may report back to the agent. " Man, they were hanging from the rafters screaming for more. This guy said he hadn't had a crowd and a reaction like that since the Stones were there in 1963. We can go back any time we like . . . but we need more bread next time, man."

The agent rings ' the guy ' immediately and learns, sadly he learns, that the group arrived late, took an hour to set up the gear, the attendance was below average, the reception was indifferent, and as they arrived late ' the guy ' expects a reduction in their fee.

Somewhere, in between, lies the truth. In between, as always, is the agent.

The group's terminology if they have gone down badly is suspiciously brief. " Oh, it was O.K. man." If that was the answer, I then knew the worst.

An agent has to nurse his attractions, constantly aware of other offices willing to sign them. Groups change their agents like a chameleon his colours, despite sole agency contracts. A rival agent may indicate his willingness to sign the group in a casual way at a social gathering. A voice, insinuating and insouciantly persuasive, whispers in the group leader's ear, " Any time you're dissatisfied, Joe, just let me know. I'm sure we can arrange a deal." If Joe is typical of most group leaders it's a certainty he's dissatisfied, ' the agent ' in his view, never ever really measuring up to the group's talents.

Contracts are issued by the booking agent and typed in

triplicate. The top copy is sent to the promoter (" Hereinafter called The Management "), the second copy to the artiste (" Hereinafter called The Artiste "), and the third copy goes into file to link with the system of contract control.

The agent hopes for a speedy return of both signatures so that he can ' exchange ', making the agreement at least technically complete. This rarely happens, both parties delaying their signature in case a better alternative transpires. Pressure from either party is heaped on the agent who has to hustle to resolve the contract he has instigated or been instructed to instigate by either of the contracting parties.

The contracts include varied stipulations worded as carefully as possible to protect the interest of the signatories. These concern methods of payment, dressing-rooms, and security and playing times. Despite careful wording of stipulations, any phraseology is open to varying interpretations and the contract that covers every contingency hasn't been, nor ever will be, drawn up. The piece of paper requires the goodwill of the signatories to make it work. Often without any deliberate intention to misread the spirit and letter of the agreement things go awry.

In the 'fifties I booked Mick Mulligan's band, through a socialite friend of George Melly's, for what is known in the business as a ' society ' gig—a twenty-first birthday party in a Mayfair mansion. It was stipulated in the contract that the hostess provided a piano. The band arrived, saw there was no piano. The hostess assured them that all was well. " Mr Godbolt is arriving with the piano at nine o'clock," she said, and George relished the vision of me struggling up that elegant staircase with a grand piano.

Sometimes it is a battle of wits between leader and promoter. In the days of the large dance band, contracts would stipulate the number of musicians—usually fifteen. The personnel in some of the lesser names were often recruited on the morning of the engagement from Archer Street, near Piccadilly, the open air ' club ' and unofficial unemployment bureau of the professional musician in those far-off days.

Often the fixer-cum-road manager failed to complete his required number by the time the coach departed, especially if it was an early call. Don Kingswell was road manager for a well-known touring band. Amongst his tasks was the job of checking the door receipts, this band invariably being on a percentage deal, usually sixty per cent of the gross receipts, sometimes against a guaranteed sum.

One night Don, no musician, played trombone, or seemed to. The leader was aware that the promoter would draw attention to the orchestra being one player short and possibly make a deduction from their share of the receipts. He instructed Don to pick up a trombone, stand alongside the other trombonists and go through the motions of playing, including some tricky manipulation with a variety of mutes. The manager out of sight, Don dropped the trombone and rushed to the door to check the takings, the bandleader not trusting the promoter to make an honest return.

If an agent has, say, eight groups working at least four nights a week that amounts to 1,500 bookings a year. Most agents have clients whose bookings could add to that figure considerably. The figures are relative—it could be more or less, but they convey some idea of the vast amount of paper work involved in the exercise.

The overheads, the furies of competition and the tensions of an unstable business, the agent accepts as part of the job for which he expects to receive his dues, but many groups have a pronounced reluctance to pay their commission, some taking the view that their trips up and down the motorways playing in crummy halls and dining in roadside greasehouses provides the agent with an easy living. However, they omit to reinforce this belief by settling their commission accounts.

When groups fail to make payment the agent will contrive to have monies sent to his office and strike a balance, a stratagem that doesn't always meet with the approval of the group. Agents owed a lot of money by artistes are not too fussy about the niceties of the law when possession is nine points of it.

Some group leaders attempt to borrow from the agent, reasoning that if he expects to earn out of the group, why shouldn't he lend the leader a little money to enable them to buy better equipment and transport to ensure punctual arrival at engagements? With all this going for the group, repayments would be speedy. It was like asking the donkey to dance a fandango before being dangled the carrot.

I knew one such honey-tongued leader with this persuasive approach. An extremely plausible rogue, he wanted £300, a figure he regarded, in 1960, as a mere trifle. Hadn't I that much faith in a group of their calibre and my own booking ability to risk a paltry £300 . . .?

I didn't fall for this soft sell and he departed forlornly protesting that the bailiffs were due to enter the following day to remove his instruments and furniture. He has since moved from one awkward financial situation to another, blithely gliding on a fluffy cloud of insolvency.

The agent is charged with collection of monies. Strictly this is the manager's job but the manager's view, and it has some logic, is that if the agent is talking to promoters and other agents daily he can easily chase up settlement. There is more to it than the application of logic. Unless the agent collects that money he doesn't get his commission.

Most offices attempt to obtain settlement on a monthly basis and unless carefully watched, commission accounts become a massive tangle. Again, there are many variables. Some promoters will deduct their agent's commission ' at source ' (on the night of the engagement). Sometimes they deduct the full ten per cent and forward the amount, although not always promptly. Sometimes they forward the entire fee to their agent, and agents capitalize themselves by unduly retaining these payments. Not that the promoter always settles without a fight.

In the 'fifties and the mid 'sixties there was a crooked promoter whom I shall call Leary O'Brian. He was infamous for his pathological inability to make settlement, for the ingenuity of his delaying tactics and for the infinite variety of imaginative excuses he employed when pressed to settle.

" WHAT! You haven't had my cheque yet? *Really?* I signed it three days ago. By gum, I'll give my secretary a bollocking when she comes in. Half a mo! Here she is now. Maisie!"

Ostensibly he turned away from the mouthpiece, but fully aware I could hear every word. " Maisie, did you post Godbolt's cheque? You did? That's all right, dear, I know you've been very busy." Now, full volume back to me. " Hello, Jim.

Still there? Maisie posted it yesterday. She didn't have time to do a letter when I signed it. Let me know if it doesn't arrive tomorrow. How are you, anyway? Business good? Hell, *we've* been snowed under."

Invariably the cheque didn't arrive on the morrow and another call involving more time and expense was made to this chiseller.

"NO! Don't tell me it hasn't arrived! Bloody G.P.O.! What?! Look, if you don't believe me I'll read you the counter-foil number." He would read out any number that came into his scheming mind.

We used to refer to "Leary O'Brian's Post" (Mick Mulligan coined the term) a lamentable service selectively inefficient when it came to the delivery of mail containing cheques.

I had been fairly successful in building up a string of clients and battled hard to keep them happy. They included private promoters, clubs and universities, but my retention of these was often put at risk by the non-arrival of groups.

The effects of non-appearance are accelerative. The crowd loses faith in the promoter's ability to support his advertising. They are not interested in excuses. In outlying districts they often travel several miles and are unimpressed with stories of breakdowns, mechanical or mental.

As the week-ends neared I used to do the telephonic rounds of offices from whom I had booked groups sniffing out poten-tial disaster, for which I acquired quite a nose. It was extra-ordinary the number of times I rang my man to be told, for instance, that the group were on the Continent and had been delayed for some reason or another. There followed anxious calls to other offices for a replacement, followed by apologetic contact with the client who didn't always fancy the replacements offered, or the price, and frequently enquired "Why this palaver? A contract's a contract, isn't it?"

In the meantime the agent I had rung could have been in touch to advise that the group *might* be O.K. to play the job. Right up to the last minute another group could be standing by, the client quite uncertain what group was going to appear on his stage.

The merry-go-round went dizzily round.

Good clients are eagerly pursued by agents. They are hard to come by and when, as sometimes happens, one comes out of the blue and proclaims, " I want you to do all my bookings," the warning signals flash bright red. Manna doesn't fall about an agent's head. They've never been in line for this special benediction. This character is likely to be a phony, a knocker—one who doesn't pay up. It's more than likely that other agents have been approached and used, to their disadvantage.

One of this kind approached me. I smelt the blue duck, made enquiries and discovered he was a heavyweight boxer who had marched into an office and threatened to break the agent's back. I didn't regard this possibility as a normal occupational hazard and declined his business.

I had grim experience of individuals recklessly booking without capital reserves. A typical example was a young lady who phoned me enquiring availabilities.

" Is X available on 25th March for a gig at Loughton, and how much?"

" They are available and the fee will be £300 for a one hour spot."

" That's cool. We'll have them. You represent Y and Z as well, don't you? Are they available? They are? That's cool, we'll have them as well."

Again, I got the warning signals. I had become what is known in the agency business as aggro-conscious. One was, to put it mildly, a little wary, perhaps a trifle cynical. I could almost hear the ominous ring of the reverse charge call as the groups arrived to find there was no promotion, or not getting paid if there was.

I asked for ' money up front '—payment in advance.

" That's cool," replied the young lady. " But I'll have to ask my friend. ELSIE! Guy at the agency wants bread up front for the groups on the 25th. That's cool isn't it?" Elsie, as it happened, didn't think it was cool. No deal, but I saved myself a lot of aggro in unnecessarily issuing contracts, the date wasn't blocked for other enquiries and I almost certainly avoided a fight for settlement.

A cheeky fellow rang me to quote for lesser-priced groups to appear in a series of promotions he was running. I had no trouble in offering him a host of these, and added I would like to book him some of the bigger attractions.

" Sorry," he said blandly. " I book these with the Harold Davison office. I wouldn't think of dealing with anyone else for the big stuff."

My reply as to what he could do with his enquiries for the small fry was succinct. It came to the heart of the matter with a quite brutal economy of words.

' Money up front ' is mandatory practice when dealing with foreign promoters. At the risk of sounding chauvinistic, the foreign promoter is a lot more crooked than the worst of his English counterparts, primarily because he knows he's safe across the water from legal action.

Just to look at a London lawyer costs a fiver and to sue a promoter in, say, Milan, would assuredly cost more than the amount involved.

When a Continental enquiry is received the agent throws the book at the enquirer. Full payment, air tickets, hotel reservations and itinerary—all two months in advance, or no deal. In this way the agent at least saves himself the reverse charge from abroad, calls that are particularly harrowing. When one heard a foreign telephone operator struggling with the English language—and with a name like mine—the blood ran cold.

Until I learned my lesson I made some expensive errors of judgement in foreign affairs with promoters and groups. I loaned one group a substantial sum to make the journey to Copenhagen. I never saw or heard from them again.

I used to think there should be some trust in business. Not any more. Should I ever be seized with some ghastly aberration and return to the agency business not one decimal tiddler will be prised from my clenched fists, the most touching appeal will not reach my stony heart. A lot is heard about crooked agents exploiting artistes—not so much when it's the other way about which, in my experience, was frequently the case.

Foreign negotiations take more time than most and when these protracted haggles were in progress I admit I played the duplicity game, played by all agents. I accepted U.K. bookings as a reserve in case the foreign negotiation foundered.

It wasn't always a case of complete deceit. Sometimes the home promoter was informed of foreign options, but it was often good politics if bad ethics not to be frank about alternatives.

With a dozen or so offices booking similar groups and all manipulating the parts in the same way, it conveys some idea of the picture of daily confusion and pretence that was the norm. On occasions like these some English promoters urgently pressing for signature would proceed with their advertising without the required signature and blame the group when they failed to appear.

These machinations sometimes resulted in the group being without work in the period set by for the foreign trip. Agents walk this sort of tight-rope as a matter of course. They have to, like it or not.

Promoters are many and varied, some part, some full time, operating in Town Halls and Corn Exchanges, some are private dance hall owners (few of these left), or a multiple chain like Mecca. Some are entertainment managers in city corporations, recreational officers in industry, officers in service establishments and cabaret clubs, these mostly in the North and Midlands.

In recent years a new kind of promoter has arisen. He is the social secretary in colleges and universities. In the *Melody Maker*, it was reported that in the year 1972, £3,000,000 was the staggering sum of campus turnover in entertainment, making them the biggest single consumer in the entertainment business. As it is virtually the only facet of the business where 100 per cent attendance is assured, where payment is equally certain, agents eagerly pursue this business.

The social secretary, a student and probably impecunious, holds office for a year during which time a stream of agents and managers lay siege at his door. He quickly realizes that he holds a position of power. In 1962 I booked for a college in North Wales. I never ever met the secretary and pleased with my booking services, he sent me a tin of cigarettes one Christmas, which Don Kingswell and John Chilton puffed away in a couple of days.

Nowadays, with a vastly increased turnover, the traffic in goods moves the other way. I recall one young man, newly elected as secretary, who did the rounds of every London agent's office and was wined and dined by all until he established the highest bidder for the pleasure of being his sole agent for his term of office.

However, the agent has no guarantee that the secretary will not swop allegiance half way during his term of office, as the latter could not sign a contract binding him to one agent, nor is the agent's ' contribution ' in gifts and cash completed when the deal is made.

I had several university clients and I entertained them as I would any other client, but never offered bribes. Many who did burnt their fingers. Their ' investment ' was greater than their commission gain.

Those who ' invested ' overcame the poor returns of split commission by ' buying and selling '—that is, negotiate a certain figure and sell at a profit. As these deals didn't entail ' splitting ' commission, agents were not averse to such arrangements. It was a far from pretty and often intricate web we all helped to weave.

Not that agents are the only crafty operators. One girl secretary at a teachers' training college skipped, in a quite Narkoverian way, with the night's takings and the college principal disclaimed all responsibility in the ensuing rumpus.

It's only fair to add that the majority of secretaries were honourable individuals and I am grateful to those who retained my services despite undoubted temptations to do otherwise.

The manager in the pop group jungle plays an entirely different role from the agent. He has the group, individually and collectively, under contract, helps shape their musical policy, directs the timing and packaging of their record releases, attends to the accounts, transportation and staff (secretaries, roadies etc.), liaises with (or employs) a press officer and usually, as in Gerry Bron's case, produces their records and owns the company through which they are released, and the company that publishes their compositions, together with all the parts tied up under his direct control to project the group efficiently.

He has to be a tough bargainer, a strong personality and almost wholly occupied with his charges and, considering the age and temperament of these bloods, he requires a special aptitude to coalesce their talents, especially in a scene where groups flutter up and die like mayflies on a summer's night.

It's significant that he never cumbers himself with actual bookings, this grinding chore delegated to an outside agent or his own agency division, and is often quite tough with the agent/booker, pushing him hard to obtain maximum fees and multiple stipulations, often leading to management/agent disputes.

Managerial identification often transcends financial considerations. He often floats on the same ego-cloud and the agent is the whipping boy if he has the temerity to question the group's asking price and the many contractual stipulations.

As an agent/booker I was often driven to distraction by the demands of managers but, on reflection, I realize they were only doing their job. In a tough, competitive game they had to pull every string, and although I think the agent should receive more for his efforts, a manager is entitled to recoup. To risk capital on and have daily contact with the gentlemen of pop warrants the larger reward.

An agent's overheads, like any other businessman's, are daily spiralling but, unlike most businessmen, he is never certain if he's going to retain the products he's currently selling, nor is there any certainty that the same product will be saleable twelve months hence. In the meantime his chances of profit are constantly bedevilled with the succession of time-wasting aggros.

I'm not suggesting that agents don't make a profit, or that they are saintly souls. Some shamelessly concentrate on the more profitable groups.

The agent can be negligent. My worst mistake resulted in a band travelling 270 miles for an engagement. The date was the only one available to the bandleader that week, it was his choice to make the journey. They arrived to find the day and venue as given in the contract but the date was out by seven rather crucial days.

Although not technically liable, it was my moral obligation to make settlement, not that the bandleader's attitude left me much choice. Members of the band were also forthcoming in their opinions about my oversight.

Despite fierce competition, most agents co-operate whenever possible, if only for their self interest. " He owes me a favour " is a favourite saying in the business. But there are exceptions and I had a few adversaries. There was one who firmly demanded that I didn't ring him first thing in the morning as he didn't like " vinegar on his cornflakes ".

One young man—he will probably end up a millionaire but in an early grave—rang to enquire availability of my groups. I automatically enquired the town and venue but this aspirant tycoon, tarring me with the same brush with which he had bedaubed himself, obviously feared that if he gave me this information I might approach the promoter direct and save paying him five per cent if a booking resulted. After persistent questioning he cautiously divulged that the venue was in the " London area ". " A sizeable expanse," I replied, " having, if you are referring to Greater London, an approximate area of 640 square miles. Now, *where* in London?" There was a pause. " Maidstone," he said almost inaudibly, as though he hoped I wouldn't hear.

" Maidstone!" I exclaimed. " Not by any stretch of the imagination could Maidstone, Kent, be described as part of the Great Wen. Given the population explosion and our increasing longevity a few more years to gather force, the London area could tragically spread from Birmingham at one end to South-ampton at the other, and all points east and west, but, at the moment, I can't possibly accept Maidstone as being in the London area, and why couldn't you have told me this in the first place?"

All this verbosity was to enjoy a little sport with an unlikeable young sharpie, to whom words of more than two syllables came as something of a puzzle. I think it was the reference to " the Great Wen " or maybe " increasing longevity " that phased him. He rang off with a snort of annoyance. Later he tried again with the same mystery approach. This time I came straight to the point. He never approached me again. If he wanted one of our groups, he would ask for Don, or get a colleague of his to ring.

The pursuit of profit makes for odd bedfellows, and I found my-self associating with someone whose bullying, hectoring personae and neighing laugh I couldn't stomach, but he was at most of the usual jazz haunts and not to be avoided. In one of these

M

places he was in argument with George Melly who invited him to step outside the premises and fight. In my cups, I volunteered to accompany them and see fair play as the invited party had often boasted about his methods of dealing with adversaries. This admirable intention, admittedly born of drink, was not put to test. When all three of us got outside the invited party turned back protesting that he didn't "trust either of us". Much to my relief Melly didn't pursue the matter. Neither of us were much versed in the noble art.

In the limited confines of the jazz scene our paths crossed and I did some deals with him, the prospect of making some money triumphing over my personal objections.

We went to Manchester to negotiate a contract. My presence was quite unnecessary. He was the dominant partner in the arrangement and did all the talking, but he wanted company, an essential constantly eluding him and I wanted money, an essential continually eluding me.

The business over, we had several drinks and fell into a dubious night club on the town's outskirts, near a canal.

We were joined by two young ladies. At least, they looked reasonably young in the club's dim lighting. Drink lent enchantment to the view nearest me and we went to her room in a 'hotel' arrived at after a round trip of the city by taxi, a con arrangement with the driver, I suspected.

After a lot to drink and a lengthy taxi ride there was a considerable build-up in my bladder and on arriving at the foyer I was bursting for a pee. There was a further hold-up as the girl insisted that the proprietor saw that we were signed in, presumably to present the appearance of respectability to this establishment. In the not so dim lighting of the 'hotel' foyer, and having sobered up a bit, the view was infinitely less enchanting and I hardly looked my romantic best writhing about, my bladder protesting for relief.

The upshot of these factors, collectively unconducive to romance, was total carnal failure. I made what I thought to be a generous settlement, bearing in mind the circuitous taxi ride, and tumbled into the street, narrowly avoiding falling into the canal, with my ego, funds and mid member (particularly) much depressed.

I walked what seemed for miles before I got a cab and was lucky to have just enough to pay the driver. Back at the hotel I thankfully slumped into bed, but (just my luck) my associate made his return a minute or two afterwards.

I feigned sleep, but he shook me and boomed, " Well, how did you get on then?"

" Brewer's Droop," I replied and pulled the bedclothes over my head.

" Hard luck," he chortled. " Mine was a cracker! Marvellous shag. She said I was the best she'd ever had and gave me my money back."

I groaned in sheer disbelief. A Manchester whore returning her fee to *him* . . . the mind boggled. But he wasn't finished.

" On the way back here a car drew up with two marvellous dollies in the back. The guy asked me to jump in. ' We'll go back to my flat and have a session,' he said. ' Which do you prefer? The wife or her sister?' I had the wife. What a grind! Hell, I'm shagged out, must get some sleep."

Which is more than I got. His snoring, at first a quivering whisper, gradually developed into a wall-shuddering crescendo. After an hour of this thunderous din I couldn't bear it any more and I made for the door, taking my mattress with me. I squeezed through a constricted passage, aiming for the furthermost point, the bathroom, but couldn't negotiate the mattress through its narrow doorway.

I settled for the corridor and was at least separated from this heaving beast by the thickness of the door, but throughout the night I was frequently awakened, despite a bellyful of drink, by the monstrous volume rising and falling from within.

When morning came he opened the door to get to the bathroom and stepped over me without a single word of enquiry or expression of surprise as to why I should have picked up my bed and walked. Obviously it was no new experience to him. If it was he hadn't the grace to apologize.

He had a good business brain, the manners of a hog and an utter contempt for human values. He later screwed me up without mercy, but I only had myself to blame. I held a candle to the devil for the sake of profit. I'm not the only sinner in this regard, and that's some sort of consolation.

14

THE VISITORS

In the mid 'fifties, after intense campaigning from the musical papers, principally the *Melody Maker*, the Musicians Union relented sufficiently to agree to a limited exchange of bands between America and Britain, operated mainly by impresario Harold Davison whose persistence and business acumen helped make the scheme a possibility. In some cases it was only just in time. Many who came over were in their last years and sadly some were past their best.

It's perhaps difficult for the non-jazz person to understand this obsession with American jazz musicians, but it was they who shaped the music that became internationally acknowledged and revered. The pride of original jazz creativeness and the romance of their history belong to them alone.

The Musicians Union official who expressed the opinion that trumpeter Kenny Baker was as good as Louis Armstrong was one who couldn't grasp the essential difference between the special qualities and ethos that separated these two musicians, both playing trumpet, both jazzmen. Jazz lovers want the original as much as an art lover.

Before the ban was lifted a client of mine conceived the notion of promoting Louis Armstrong's All-Stars on a ship three miles outside the coast-line, thus removing the event from the inevitable interference of the Musicians Union and their running hounds, the Ministry of Labour. It was an outlandish, ill-considered scheme but illustrated to what lengths certain promoters would go to meet the almost desperate desire of jazz lovers to hear American musicians in this country and, in the case of Bert Wilcox with Sidney Bechet, flagrantly breaking the law.

I was obliged to make enquiries about Armstrong's fees and availabilities. His agent in this country was Sir (then plain Mr) Lew Grade. Phoning early in the morning, I actually managed to speak to this tycoon but was given short shrift—and without my mentioning that the performance would be on a ship. " If you're an agent," he snapped, " stop wasting my time," and rang off.

It wasn't only the lay jazz public who desperately wanted the Americans over here. There were critics and discographers eager to question them. At the time of the Bechet concert, Louis Armstrong set foot in this country, en route with his All-Stars to play a festival in Nice.

It was a golden opportunity for zealous aficionados to actually talk to these idols. Amongst the host of worshippers who arrived at London Airport was an intrepid journalist and collector determined to discover if Louis had played on an obscure record made in 1930 called " Blue Yodel No. 9 " recorded by hill-billy singer, Jimmie Rodgers.

The journalist was Max Jones, who brought a wind-up gramophone to the V.I.P.'s room, sat before an astonished Armstrong, played him the record and asked verification, or otherwise, of Louis's presence. It was a unique situation. Here was a major artiste of our time, with an international reputation, confronted by a journalist armed with a portable gramophone and a box of steel needles.

Louis declared he was on the record and another entry went firmly into the Armstrong discography. The *Melody Maker* proudly headlined their " Collectors Corner " column (a page devoted purely to jazz) " CORNER SCOOPS WORLD ON 1930 ARMSTRONG DISC ".

My old friend Max is one of the most lovable characters on the British jazz scene despite his unequalled capacity for talking non-stop. As a result of a nervous affliction in the mid 'forties he lost all his hair and constantly wears a beret—twiddled with the nervous rapidity of his sentences. Acknowledged as one of the world's authorities on jazz, he has interviewed more jazzmen than any other journalist in this country and written several scholarly books on the music he passionately loves.

The case that a limited entry of American jazz musicians would *make* work for British jazz musicians was proven during the 1960s when Harold Davison brought over solo musicians to play tours supported by British bands. My office co-promoted these tours and Don looked after the visitors.

To meet and talk with these heroes of mine was a thrill, a dream come true. Don mocked this adulation and threw a few barbs about " fuddy-duddy fan worship ". I had no retort, except to say that I was grateful for those whose playing had given me such deep and abiding pleasure, whose records had changed my life and, indeed, set its very pattern.

When John Chilton and I used to discuss these musicians and their discographies with obvious, perhaps adolescent-like enthusiasm, the Kingswell jowls wobbled in disbelief.

" *You* people! You make me laugh! You and your scratchy old 78s!" He mockingly invented his own ' discographal ' figure, one Matthews, whose instrument Don changed from week to week but who, according to Kingswell, recorded for the Regal-Zonophone label in 1926.

" Great player, Matthews! Really socks out the blues. Can't wait to get home and play his 78s. An evening of Matthews really knocks me and The Enemy right out!" The Regal-Zonophone label didn't exist in 1926, but it had sufficiently antique associations to support Don's barbs.

It was this lack of interest in jazz that, paradoxically, endeared him to the visiting jazz musicians. He didn't bug them with ceaseless questions about their past, and protected them from those who wished to. This questioning of veteran jazz musicians is one of their occupational hazards and one player, trombonist Vic Dickenson, actually fled a hall to lock himself in a car and escape his questioners.

Some of the visitors had no objections to answering questions. Many were amazed at the knowledge displayed by collectors. Trumpeter Bill Coleman was puzzled that a record of a German popular singer of the 'thirties, Greta Keller, was being played to him by collector John Kendal until, to his astonishment, he realized he was in the accompanying band. He had completely forgotten he was on the session.

A lot depended on the questioner's approach. Some harked

back to a past the musicians wanted to forget, some couldn't accept that styles had changed, and wanted only to hear reproductions of solos recorded by these musicians twenty, maybe thirty years earlier.

I should have known better but I ploughed in with references to the past without first sounding out the subject's willingness to talk. I was having a drink with tenor saxophonist Bud Freeman before he appeared at the ' Bull's Head ', Barnes, and I mentioned I had been listening to records he had made with violinist Joe Venuti in 1933.

He froze. " *We* don't discuss those *old* records. They were made *so* long ago. *Now* if you could hear the discs I made with two guitars *last* year . . ." At that moment Sinclair Traill, editor of Britain's longest established jazz magazine, *Jazz Journal*, and a close friend of the Honourable Gerald Lascelles, appeared at the door and Freeman, for all his sixty years, bounded away like a young gazelle, leaving me, and my observations about 1933, for dead—probably to discuss some aspect of the British monarchy, Bud being a devout admirer of the Royal Family.

One visitor was quite forthcoming but didn't have too favourable an impression of England. " Too many niggers on the sidewalk " was one of his pronouncements, an odd comment from a man who frequently boasted about his friendship with Louis Armstrong. But he was professional in his approach, and played well.

There were other visitors whose behaviour was extremely unprofessional and often played very badly. My dream of meeting so many legendary figures often became a living nightmare and many of the romantic images nurtured over the years were unhappily destroyed after some hair-raising experiences with idols who had feet of clay, and were in some cases over fond of strong drink.

One tenor saxophonist, Don Byas, carried an obscene litany which every young lady fortunate enough to know the joy of his passion was obliged to read first. This selection of odes was but one unsavoury feature of an abrupt, aggressive and unlovely person. Don Kingswell, genial and anxious to please, introduced himself. He told Byas his job was to look after him throughout the tour and mentioned that a previous tour by saxophonist Ben Webster had been spoilt by Ben's excessive drinking.

Byas assured Don that he, unlike Webster, could take his drink. Kingswell, reassured, mentioned that Webster had carried a big knife. He was further relieved that Byas appeared to respond with incredulous disbelief. He soon discovered why.

"You don't say!" exclaimed Byas. "A big knife, huh? You call that thing Ben had a big knife? That was nuthin'. Look at this, man. Now *here's* a *big* knife," and as he spoke he drew a fearsome-looking dagger from his belt. Don backed away in understandable fright.

Ben Webster sober was a reasonable person and played marvellously. Drunk, he was aggressive and played badly. One night he surpassed himself by striding, naked and unashamed, through a hotel corridor brandishing his knife and tried to obtain entry into a ladies' toilet where his girlfriend was hiding.

He had a penchant for ladies' toilets. He repeated his attempt to gain entry into one at a U.S. serviceman's club in London when his lady friend again fled to safety.

This was a dramatic finale to a phantasmagoric evening. The accompanying band had a fine piano player who was also a renowned soak. With him and Webster both very drunk, the proceedings soon degenerated into a fiasco. When he wasn't actually playing, Webster was haranguing his girl; the pianist was all but slumped over the keyboard; and the rest of the band, understandably, were hardly playing their best.

Don Kingswell, helpless in the circumstances, was buttonholed by the club's secretary, a beefy master sergeant, who pointed to the pianist's condition. Don assured him that the pianist's demeanour indicated total concentration in his playing. As he spoke, the pianist's head hit the keyboard with a resounding crash, producing a cluster of splintered chords that had no relation to the tune he was attempting to play.

"It was phantasglorium," said Don the following day. "Absolute bloody *phantasglorium*!" The club paid only half the contracted fee. I could hardly blame them. They had booked a jazz package and got a 'phantasglorium' instead.

Webster was not without a gallant side to his nature. He solemnly assured Max Jones that if anyone were to take liberties with his attractive wife, Betty, the knife would be used to teach the fellow a sharp lesson. I imagine Max twiddled his beret even more rapidly than usual.

I had an unhappy experience with Ben when he was rehearsing with Bruce Turner's band. Normally I don't say a word at rehearsals, but Bruce was seemingly struck dumb and the pianist was struggling with unfamiliar tunes Ben wanted to play. I unwisely stepped in and suggested that Ben play some numbers with the band and give the pianist a chance to study the chords. Webster agreed in a surly fashion and still Bruce remained silent. Having previously discussed the programme with Bruce, I prompted him and Webster savagely turned on me. " Do you *mind*!" he snarled. " Let the man speak."

When Ben Webster was aroused his expression was alarmingly malevolent. I immediately retired to a corner and when a brief and scrappy rehearsal was over Ben, a paunchy, shambling man, lumbered over to me and in a tone supercharged with sarcasm asked if the rehearsal had been O.K. by me. Now thoroughly chastened I mumbled assent.

" Oh, that's *fine*," he said. " As long as it's O.K. by *you*," and shambled away to talk to a friend. His voice floated over. " You're right, man. He was a fool, but there's always a fool about." He didn't have to look in my direction, nor did I have to be paranoiac to appreciate that I was the person he immediately had in mind.

Later I rang him to apologize for what seemed to be interference. It took him some time to connect me with the person he had rubbished that afternoon. Perhaps he had seen a few more off since. I explained that I only wanted to be of assistance.

" That's O.K. man. I understand, but you must remember I've been rehearsing musicians for ninety-nine years." Point taken and lesson learned.

Later we had a rough passage with another soak. We had been warned about this ' drunky-punky ', to use Don's pungent description, but when he arrived at my office he looked fit and spruce for someone in his late fifties and an alleged alcoholic.

He was charming and fully co-operative but there was a nudging undercurrent of doubt. No one ever offered him a drink and at a dinner party given in his honour, the hostess, placed in an awkward situation, offered him only Coca-Cola when the rest of us were drinking considerably stronger beverages.

In this embarrassing conspiracy of silence no one mentioned his alleged addiction. Perhaps the matter should have been brought out into the open.

He and the band played their first dates in Switzerland, and in a café with a girl he ordered a Coca-Cola for himself. The girl made scornful reference to a jazzman taking a soft drink. This jab at his ego sparked off a disastrous train of events, and on some nights he was too drunk to play. One evening he was in a restaurant with the band and well drunk. He looked hungrily at a steak one of the band was eating, grabbed it with his hand, took a hefty bite and replaced it.

The manager of the hotel remembered him from a pre-war trip to Europe and asked his distinguished visitor to be the first to sign a brand new visitors' book. The distinguished visitor didn't realize that the pen offered him was a biro and when he failed to make it inscribe, he maniacally plunged it into a bread roll thinking it was an inkwell.

My first intimation of these disasters was a call from Don Kingswell from London Airport. He had gone to transport the star back to London, the band travelling in an opposite direction. I thought Don was kidding, having received an assuring postcard at the beginning of the tour, but his grave tone and description of our man covered in blood from a drunken fall soon convinced me otherwise.

A representative of the Davison office and myself called on this wayward star in his hotel room, a functional box, sparsely furnished for minimum requirements. His head was bandaged. The light was dim. Playing the alcoholic's deception game, he warmly greeted us, quickly told us how much he had enjoyed the tour, and what a great bunch of guys the band were.

Angry and depressed as I was, I felt sick for him. The Davison representative threatened to send him home. The visitor pleaded that the tour be continued and he promised to abstain from the drink. We departed that cheerless room. He had been a giant of jazz in his time. Now he was a pathetic wreck alone in that room.

The band, themselves renowned drinkers, were understandably fearful of their reputation and pressed that the tour be cancelled. They were persuaded to continue and my mind darted in many directions to seek a solution, even, with the optimism of the desperate, thinking he might be cured of his addiction.

I phoned the local office of Alcoholics Anonymous and spoke to an official. He thought the man whose condition I described was myself and hiding the fact. He urged me to confess my addiction. " After all, old boy, we're all in this boat together you know. It's best to come clean and we'll see what we can do to help."

I had to admit that I was conceivably in need of help but my problems were not so pressing. Only partially convinced that it was not myself, the A.A. man gave me an address of a clinic in West London. As though in a mad dream, I spoke to someone with a thick Viennese accent urging me to send the man along and he would give him a deterrent pill. He asserted that if he were foolish enough to drink alcohol after taking this the effects would be dire. He said, " 'E will turn green, I promise you."

A mental picture of a light-skinned negro turning green on taking a drink was a bizarre touch that had me reeling.

It was a tough three weeks. Our guest and band had been booked to appear on a B.B.C. show called " Jazz 625 ". The rehearsal, at the Shepherds Bush studio, was called at 11 a.m. At 11.30 I got an urgent call from a bandleader advising me to make haste to the studio. He could see our man had been drinking. I rushed to the studio and was relieved to see that he was anything but drunk (having had long experience of discerning that condition), but I was frightened that a few more snorts would put paid to the day's proceedings. I made no mention of him drinking. I tell myself to this day that I remained silent because I wanted no upsets on a show that was just one of a series with all the other U.S. visitors lined up to appear in it, but it was undoubtedly moral cowardice combined with the last vestige of hero worship that kept me quiet.

When he left the dressing-room to rehearse with the band, I

discovered a half-bottle of whisky in his instrument case. Some of it had been drunk. I was in an agonizing dilemma. If I left the whisky for him to finish this might render him incapable. If I poured it away his prop would be taken from underneath him. I temporized, and emptied half the contents down the sink, resisting the temptation to pour the lot down my gullet. I replaced the bottle on its side so that the contents might not appear to be less than when he put it down after the last life-giving sip.

It was the longest day. From the time I discovered the whisky I watched him like a cat tensed over a mousehole. I reckoned that he would see the day through as long as he *thought* he might get at that bottle. Time and time again he went to his instrument case to withdraw his instrument and give it an unnecessary polish. It was a nerve-wracking and sorrowful vigil. I made polite chat. I got morose and abrupt replies. He had one all-consuming wish—to get at the bottle.

It was the appearance of a veteran collector and his wife that could have proved our undoing. The dressing-room had two centre sliding doors. When they met the room was divided into two. The half partition nearest to me was extended and the bandleader, changing his trousers, closed the partition nearest to him to shield the lady from the spectacle.

This was the star's opportunity. In a matter of seconds he was away, with instrument case and its precious liquid contents. I searched, but with an alcoholic's cunning he had previously selected a bolt-hole and I next saw him walking down a flight of stairs with a triumphant gleam in his eyes. He'd had his taste; enough to set him up for the show.

As it happened, the show went well, but I wasn't to know this when I first discovered the drink, nor was I to know if this whisky was merely starters, and other bottles were hidden away.

I rushed to the nearest pub and, putting drinks down me with unseemly haste, muttered curses on all alcoholic jazzmen.

At the end of the show our troublesome visitor came into the dressing-room, sighed and said, " Must get some sleep. Sure has been a hard day." I was silently echoing these sentiments when he looked intently at me and said, " Think you should do the same. You kinda look all-in," and coolly, deliberately, he added,

" Guess all that liquor you been drinking won't do you much good, either."

I was rendered dumb. Had I not stood over him all day, there's no knowing what sort of shambles would have ensued, and with this breathtaking effrontery he was warning me against the evils of drink. . . .

The shambles came a few nights later at a club on the south coast. He swayed on to the stage, dropped his instrument, couldn't retrieve it, and had to be led off. There were only a few more days of the tour and the band philosophically resigned themselves to the worst.

One of the last engagements was at a West Country university. The home rugby team had won a game for the first time that season and almost all the audience, celebrating victory, were drunk. So was the guest star, but the patron saint of soaks was by his side that night. The social secretary was emphatic that he couldn't possibly allow an artiste of the star's calibre to appear before an audience so thoroughly boozed. He paid the band off with further apologies.

Propped up in a chair in the corner of the dressing-room, staring rigidly ahead with glazed, non-seeing eyes, was the artiste to whom the condition of the audience would have been an affront. He was sent home. A month or so later he sent me an allusively apologetic letter and enclosed a weird selection of good luck trinkets for Don, John Chilton, the band and myself. There was also a gift for the Davison representative. It was a particularly evil-looking glass eye, as though the sender had put the Harlem curse on this man. It showed the sender wasn't all bad!

Pianist Earl Hines, confrère of Louis Armstrong in the late 'twenties, and later with Louis's All-Stars, toured this country in 1965 with Alex Welsh's Band. We had met when he toured this country with Jack Teagarden in 1957 but, understandably, he showed no sign of recognition. Touring musicians meet thousands of people and can hardly be expected to remember every face and name, but he may recall me now, perhaps not by name, but by recollection of an unfortunate night at a club in Hampstead I was running on Friday nights.

I had booked him with Alex Welsh's excellent rhythm section, but asked if he would play a spot with some of my favourite musicians, Bruce Turner, John Picard and Sandy Brown. Hines demurred. " But why do I need other musicians—I've got ten musicians here," he said, splaying both hands to illustrate his meaning. But, reluctantly he agreed.

The session was a disaster, and for what reason I'll never know. Bruce Turner, a fine saxophonist, but low on moral fibre, was the first to leave the stand and Picard soon followed, leaving Sandy to struggle bravely, or obdurately, or both, with a quite uncooperative Hines. Sandy didn't give up. If Hines had wanted these men off the stage, he reckoned without the fortitude of Alexander Brown, F.R.I.B.A., clarinettist, composer, blues singer, writer, pianist, painter and raconteur. It was an utterly dismaying turn of events. When the number eventually came to a painful close, Hines stormed up to me. " Don't you ever dare put me on with those guys again," he yelled, and added a few steaming epithets about me. For years I had revered Hines, and at that moment I felt like departing to nearby Hampstead Heath and seeking the deepest pond.

There were other occasions, too, when I often wished that contact with my heroes had been limited to gramophone records, but I had some extremely happy experiences with some of our visitors. I cherish memories of meetings with great negro jazzmen—clarinettists Albert Nicholas and Edmond Hall, trombonist Vic Dickenson and trumpeters Red Allen, Rex Stewart and Bill Coleman.

Ed Hall was a most delightful person. We hit it off immediately we met, his playing was a joy, his behaviour impeccable. He came to my house and I showed him a photograph of himself with Buddy Petit's Band taken in New Orleans forty years earlier. He recalled the name of every player and talked freely about his career. An extremely gentle person he was nevertheless vituperative about white supremacy in the United States. He was also forthcoming about certain white jazz musicians.

On this tour he was accompanied by Alan Elsdon's Band. Returning from an engagement he expressed the opinion that the white clarinettist Pee Wee Russell " played nothin'." I ventured to disagree. A guest pianist, Lennie Felix, rounded on me

in seething fury. What right had I, a non-musician, to disagree
with a giant of jazz? Furthermore I was only a crummy agent
and all (!) the pianos in my clubs (!) were out of tune!

Ed gently remonstrated with him, but Felix couldn't restrain
his fury. I'm sure it was only the fact of Alan Elsdon seated
between us that prevented him from attacking me physically.

Before going home, Ed bought me a record he had made with
Chris Barber's band with a message written across the back of
the sleeve—and I see no reason why I shouldn't reproduce it
here. It said: "To Jim, the most efficient gentleman I ever
worked for and wishing him the best of everything."

A year later he died of a heart attack. I felt a great sadness.
I had walked with a Titan.

Another great pleasure was meeting ex-Duke Ellington trumpeter, Rex Stewart. Instrumentally Rex was past his best, but
he was an exhilarating conversationalist about jazz.

He sent me a charming letter when he returned to America.
Again, I make no apologies for reproducing this. I believe the
sentiments expressed to be genuine and any jazz lover would be
proud to receive such a letter:

"Jim, my hearty, The memory of meeting you shall long be
a pleasant glow. Homo Sapiens tend to be a common commodity
but gentlemen are rare and by your unswerving courtesy which
is an integral part of Godbolt—at least which I've seen of you—
I do attest that you are well named and it has been a pleasure
to know you, for you are a gentleman. May good attend your
ventures and I would, figuratively speaking, shake the hands of
your confrères, Don and John, a fine pair of fellows. I shall
always remember your kindness over and above the call of
duty."

Sadly he, too, has since died.

Henry 'Red' Allen, grandmaster of jazz trumpet, was a man
of immense dignity and charm. During Henry's last trip he had
a premonition that he'd not long to go but, ill as he was, and
past his prime, the superb old professional spun audacious and
unexpected phrases from his horn. Henry was also my guest for
one absorbing night and he talked freely and with incredible
detail about his long career. His death caused more genuine
mourning amongst British jazz fans than any other American

musician who has visited us—other than Louis Armstrong, of course.

Trumpeter Bill Coleman, happily still alive and still blowing marvellously at the age of seventy-two, was an extremely charming person and completely professional in his approach. It was difficult to think of him as (then) being sixty-two years of age, so outstanding was his playing. He played at the ' Six Bells ' with Bruce Turner's Band. The ' Bells ' at that time was managed by a rough diamond with a heart of gold called Bert, but Bert wasn't the most tactful of persons. In his presence, Bill Coleman was shown a photograph of himself in a jazz magazine. Bert looked intently at the photo, then at Bill and without any intention to be offensive he cried, " Why, you're not as black as that!" He closely examined Bill's light pigmentation. " Bloody cheek! Making you look as black as that!" Bill, kind and gentle, just laughed. Had Ben Webster been the subject of the photograph, we could have expected ructions.

These happy hours with great jazzmen will forever remain in my memory. I feel I was privileged to be in their company, to have entertained them as my guests, but it remains an artistic crime of some enormity that an obtuse ban existed for years when a lot of jazz greats were alive and in their prime. It was a deprivation of the rights of any person to listen to whom he wishes without first having to beg permission from a claque of obdurate bullies with closed minds and disproportionate power.

The worst experience in my entire business career was with a visiting artiste, although not a jazzman. He and his bodyguard, both negro, and his manager, Jewish, were blatantly and viciously racial in their antipathy towards Don and myself. It was a strange experience to suffer what is the daily lot of millions. Here it had disastrous effects on the tour that was to be profitable and prestigious. The component parts of six horrendous weeks turned out to be deception, blackmail, violence and bloody-mindedness.

I was contractually obliged to various parties to continue with the agony, but it was only thanks to Don's courage and patience that the tour went the full course.

At the end of a ghoulish experience the graphic Kingswell

said, "I tell you, boy, those three shithouses are rotten all through. I wouldn't piss on them if they were burning!"

A lawsuit followed and my solicitor was enthusiastic about the outcome. " I enjoy a good fight, Mr Godbolt," he said. The case never came to court, my adversary was prevailed upon to make settlement and I received a letter from my doughty solicitor, the relevant paragraph of which is as follows :

" Mr X had agreed to pay £185 from the joint account. In the view of the fact that this matter is now closed I hereby enclose my firm's bill. In fact the total costs and disbursements listed herewith amount to £189, but as you are not personally recovering any sum from the settlement the costs have been deliberately rounded off to the sum received."

Such generosity overwhelmed me! I swore I would never go into court again merely for the benefit of solicitors. This letter was an appropriate ending to a tour that was a nightmare.

N

MUSTY SMELLS OF 78s

I joined the Bron Organization in 1968 after a run of disasters due to both bad luck and faulty judgement. I was a fish in someone else's pond but had no regrets. A measure of security in an expanding organization was better than having my name on the notepaper (which it was, in the minutest of print) but after a year I was making the useless comparisons with the seemingly ugly present and a generally enjoyable past.

Increasingly and with a lot of turbulent inner feelings I was pondering—why stay in a *milieu* I didn't enjoy?

This was no criticism of Gerry Bron, one of the most gentlemanly people I've ever met in the entertainment business. I'd had enough of the lunatic fringe even when their antics didn't directly affect me. I was ashamed of being in the pop business. I remained silent about the way I earned my living. Understandably so—some of the individuals on the scene were beyond the pale.

A group's manager called to see me. He outlined their act, a feature of which was the slitting of a live chicken's throat during a 'composition' where the lyrics related to Black Mass. I earnestly assured this wretch that if I ever heard of this obscenity actually occurring I would see to it personally that he and the group would be prosecuted for unnecessary cruelty to animals.

On a more hilarious note, there was a group where the highlight of the act was the drummer leaving the stand and returning through the audience completely naked *and* with a roll of newspaper stuck up his anus. If this wasn't enough of a novelty, the end of the newspaper was alight. Leaving aside the grave dangers of a wider conflagration in a crowded hall this was indeed something different.

I thought of my heroes when I read of these extraordinary antics : Duke Ellington, for instance. If, say, the audience had been apathetic one night at the Cotton Club in New York, where he was resident for years, would he have called saxophonist Johnny Hodges aside and said, " Look, John, we're not getting much of a reaction tonight. Here's a copy of *Tribune* and a box of matches. Would you mind stripping off and . . .?"

Is this where the jazzmen of my acquaintance went wrong? Would features as arresting as this have helped make their fortunes, or retain their popularity when the Rock n' Roll bombshell hit the profession? Too late now, but I wouldn't have put it past George Melly, and I had an intriguing image of Acker quite naked except for his bowler.

Musing about this drummer exhibitionist, I thought how much I would have liked to be near when he was preparing for his big moment and surreptitiously dash some highly inflammable spirit to the paper and accelerate this act of nether incendiarism.

The outcome of this bold drummer giving the audience a full frontal was that the promoter (who had this sprung on him as an additional attraction and with no extra charge) now insists on yet another stipulation in his contracts. It's a " No Stripping " clause, heaven help us. To have seen Humphrey Lyttelton's expression reading that clause in one of his contracts would have been worth a king's ransom.

We received some intriguing literature advising another novel presentation that included a dog and a cockerel. The group obviously knew they couldn't go wrong with a dog in the act. A canine pathetically looking up would move even an audience of anti-establishment hippies. At a given signal, the dog peed against the microphone stand and the cockerel had been trained to eat corn off the top of the guitarist's head. No mention was made of what sort of music the group played. With such novel features in their act, music was obviously a minor consideration. The cockerel was dressed in red drawers.

These absurdities, and outrages, pale into insignificance beside an American rock and roll act called, simply, Alice Cooper. Alice, who has toured this country, is a male who appears in gold lamé, skin-tight trousers and black leather jacket. His eyes are ringed with mascara and a live python wriggles and undulates under his crotch. He sings, this Alice, but enlivens his act by stabbing at baby dolls, seeming to attack the drummer with broken glass, thrashes the rest of the group with a whip and the finale of this spectacle is a simulation of him being hung on stage gallows, apparently with a frightening semblance of actuality.

Not being one for gratuitous savagery in my entertainment, I haven't seen the act and these details are taken from press reports, including one by Tony Palmer in the *Observer*. Even Palmer, an eloquent apologist for pop, regards this sort of viciousness as a sinister trend, especially as others are imitating its highly dubious morality. One of these is David Bowie.

He appears with his hair dyed orange, wears lipstick, cheek glitter, false eyelashes and his various changes of stage dress include lace high-heeled shoes, flowing silk scarves and a black silk net jockstrap showing through transparent tights. He has prophesied that " Shortly a big artiste is going to get killed and I keep thinking it's going to be me ".

Alice, by the way, gives away scanty underpants when signing his record albums and those garments have been showered on to his audiences from a net above the stalls. The willingness of audiences to support acts of this kind denotes a mentality I find frightening beyond belief.

At a time when there is heavy emphasis on the beliefs and requirements of the young, when to be middle-aged appears to be some sort of sin, I am almost scared to propound a view that automatically puts me in the ageing, reactionary class but the thought occurred to me, which I courageously express here, that when Louis Armstrong and his fellow gods played their moving and poetic music (music recorded four decades ago and still avidly appreciated) did they behave like demented jackals, offer the spectacle of full frontals and rush through their audiences with lighted newspapers up their backsides? Did they include a dog peeing against the microphone stand in their act? Was there anyone in any sphere of entertainment as gross and potentially dangerous as Alice? Were films made of them whilst a member of the audience was actually murdered, as in the Rolling Stones *Gimme Shelter*?

The jazzmen who misbehaved under the influence of drink were the victims of addiction; their behaviour wasn't contrived viciousness, nor was it a part of their stage performance.

I had to remind myself that some of my contemporaries had prodigious thirsts and perhaps I am taking an unduly rosy view of these, but rarely can I recall drunkenness leading to violence, nor do I recall them stuffing toilet paper down hotel lavatories, as in a recently admitted instance of pop star behaviour by a British performer in America.

But neither American or British jazzmen were so hysterically acclaimed as these new style demi-gods, nor did they command such enormous fees. Perhaps if they had been the recipients of so much adulation and money that might have made them behave in a similar fashion. I like to think otherwise.

A necessary part of my duties at Bron's was to listen in the evening to our groups, and to others who were prospects for representation.

I didn't like this duty, a bad attitude for a booker. He must show his face when the groups make an appearance in town. They like to think that his attendance will make him all the more enthusiastic about them, but this booker couldn't, for a start, bear the inordinate volume. Whatever merits their music had were lost to me in this shattering welter of sound.

One night I went to the Marquee Club, in Wardour Street, to hear a group. Also present was a young propagandist for 'heavy rock', Nick Jones, Max's son. Nick wasn't interested in jazz, despite (or perhaps because of) intensive jazz conditioning from birth. When we began our conversation the room was quiet, but the bass guitarist alone commenced to tune his instrument with his amplifier fully turned up. I involuntarily jumped, and hastily sought comparative shelter behind a brick wall, which for all the sturdiness of its construction, trembled under the decibel impact. Nick hadn't noticed anything untoward, except my hasty movement and pained expression, both of which caused him considerable amusement. I was genuinely shaken, almost as if I had been shot at, and railed against the insensate volume.

"The trouble with you, Godbolt," said Nick, "is that you've still got the musty smell of 78s about you."

How true, how very pleasurably true! How happy to acknowledge the fact. How very pleased that I've long enjoyed Duke Ellington, Louis Armstrong, Bix Beiderbecke, Coleman Hawkins, Jack Teagarden, Sidney Bechet and Ed Hall and their fellow giants, whose music came to us on the 78 rpm record.

This is music that will be listened to forever, unlike, I'm sure, the grotesque rock and roll that has to be belted at its listeners through amplifiers of monstrous power.

Ordinary conversation in clubs like the Marquee was quite impossible when the groups were playing. To make oneself heard it was necessary to peer close into people's waxy earholes and shout hard. Any attempt to speak more than a sentence or two was a strain on the larynx.

To me jazz has grace, dignity and beauty. Excitement is not its only characteristic. Rock and roll is excessively loud, frenetic and shallow. Jazz and rock and roll both are products of this century, but the latter now has a strong connection with the harsh, abrasive society in which we now live.

Even with the financial security at Bron's, I was becoming increasingly tetchy about the aggravations, disliking more and more the overall atmosphere of the business, even more reluctant to listen to the music I was selling. An old anxiety neurosis returned. At the end of the day the inside of my mouth was raw from compulsive biting.

As I was on commission and, I like to think, a conscientious person, I hoped that my personal feelings didn't affect my booking approach, but perhaps these innermost thoughts showed through the surface enthusiasm. In any case, this play-acting was becoming wearisome, even for money. Money speaks all languages, opens most doors, and soothes most pains, but it can't obliterate truths and one of these was that I was something of an anachronism in the rock and roll scene. The musty smell of 78s didn't blend too well with some of the more malodorous aspects of the business.

During one lunch break I bumped into my former dentist in Soho Square, off Oxford Street. I asked him where he was practising. " I'm not, old boy. Finished with dentistry. Got fed up with peering down people's horrible mouths—er, excepting yours, of course, old boy."

This reply helped to crystallize my feelings. I was fed up with peering at horrible date sheets. After long years of darting from one sheet to another, from this query to that problem, I had developed the mind of a grasshopper. I couldn't even read a newspaper without jumping paragraphs and to read a book involved a massive application of will-power.

In what may seem a superior manner, I was weary of the monosyllabic grunts that passed for conversation amongst so many performers and their representatives. I was sick of having my ear drums rattled, having to scream hard to make simple comment at rock clubs. I was tired of the posturing and un-reliability of egocentric idols.

I realized it was time to quit. Then (1970) I was nudging fifty, a middle-aged jazz buff in a business where I had seen many changes and helped to ring some of them. I can claim to have been a hard-working, reasonably honest agent, even though I have been involved in deals I'm hardly proud of. I had kept my head above water for twenty years, but I had been without the driving ambition and financial acumen to really succeed as a business man. I realized that my energies had often been misdirected, my funds dribbled away on useless projects. And—no humbug—had I been making a fortune, no doubt I would have stayed in the business, whatever the aggravations. That's what belonging to the rate race means.

I'd had my moments and a lot of laughs. I had met an incred-ible variety of people and made some highly valued friends.

I had long wanted to try my hand at writing, having no illusions about the fact that this could be as frustrating as the agency business and certainly worse paid; but I hoped I might find it more fulfilling. At least when a piece of writing is finished there is a sense of *completion*, a feeling I never had as an agent/ booker dealing with forever open-ended date sheets.

I had moved into a flat near Hampstead Heath, itself a sweet heritage, a little pocket of almost rural peace in the frightening conurbation of Greater London. The flat, five floors up, had a sun balcony with a southern aspect and overlooked peaceful gardens. To work from here, especially during the summer, seemed infinitely preferable to the din and pollution of the West End and the machinations of commerce.

This prospect struck me with particular force after I left the dentist and walked into Oxford Street, where the Bron Organization had its offices. This litter-strewn thoroughfare is a vision of hell on earth to come. Thousands of people, many with tense expressions, were jostling for space. Dense traffic jerking forward in fits and starts was emitting a clearly visible purple haze of poisonous carbon monoxide.

The October sun was still summer-warm and above the canyon of shops and offices, I could see a strip of blue sky. I decided to get out of the business as soon as possible. It was a Thursday and I went to see Gerry to ask if I could leave the following day. We were still in the summer recess and my sudden departure would cause no inconvenience. Gerry, an understanding person, accepted my immediate resignation.

On the following night I went to hear Jon Hiseman's Coloseum—a group I had booked at Bron's. They played under a vast screen on which stroboscopes projected dazzling, sometimes eerily beautiful images. Jon, a very nice person, announced my retirement from the business to a palpably uninterested audience. I suspect they thought he was announcing a new number with a weird title, but it signalled the end of my involvement with pop music, and the entertainment business generally.

The next day I played cricket with the Ravers in our one country-house fixture at Great Martins, Waltham St Lawrence, Berkshire. I made sixteen runs, not out, took a good catch in the deep, and for the first time in twenty years felt as free as the song birds flitting around this lovely ground.

That night I went to the 100 Club where, by sheer coincidence, Humphrey Lyttelton was guesting with a Manchester trad band and blowing as he did those twenty-three years earlier with George Webb's Dixielanders. George Webb was himself present and sat in on a few numbers. Beryl Bryden sang. This, I thought, is almost where I came in. The following week the *Melody Maker* had a few lines in their gossip column, " The Raver ", reporting that I had quit the business and would have " more time to devote to my Miff Mole L.P.s."

Miff Mole! Now, that's really where I came in, at the 161 Rhythm Club, Sidcup, Kent, thirty years previously, and I wondered whatever happened to that young lady who had fled during Frank Teschmaker's solo on Miff's record of " Shim-Me-Sha-Wobble " when she saw the spider crawling down the wall. It was an odd thought on which to end thirty years' association with the music business.

INDEX

Page numbers in bold figures indicate a facing illustration